Modern American Manners

Modern American Manners

DINING ETIQUETTE FOR HOSTS AND GUESTS

FRED MAYO AND MICHAEL GOLD

Skyhorse Publishing

BJ2041.M396 2017x
Mayo, Frederic B., author.
Modern American manners :
dining etiquette for hosts
and guests
New York, NY : Skyhorse
Publishing, [2017]

Skyhorse Publishing books may be purchased in bulk at special discounts for sales promotion, corporate gifts, fund-raising, or educational purposes. Special editions can also be created to specifications. For details, contact the Special Sales Department, Skyhorse Publishing, 307 West 36th Street, 11th Floor, New York, NY 10018 or info@skyhorsepublishing.com.

Skyhorse® and Skyhorse Publishing® are registered trademarks of Skyhorse Publishing, Inc.®, a Delaware corporation.

Visit our website at www.skyhorsepublishing.com.

10 9 8 7 6 5 4 3 2 1

Library of Congress Cataloging-in-Publication Data is available on file.

Cover design by Rain Saukas

Print ISBN: 978-1-5107-1765-7
Ebook ISBN: 978-1-5107-1767-1

Printed in China

This book is dedicated to my parents—Anne and Fred Mayo—who taught me about hosting, generosity, kindness in daily life, and manners at the dining table; to my sisters—Pinny Randall, Joie Mayo, and Dorothy Klima—with whom I learned table manners as a child; and to my children—Beth Routledge and David Wightman—who showed me how much fun it can be to teach and practice manners.

Fred Mayo
New Paltz, New York
November 2016

Dedicated to my greatest loves—Linnie, my incredible, beautiful, supportive wife; Gabrielle and Arianne, my extraordinary, loving daughters; Juniper and Magnolia, the smartest, most beautiful granddaughters in the world; Ethan, my terrific, athletic, smart, sweet grandson; and Dane and Charlie, the best sons-in-law one could be lucky enough to simply call sons.

Michael Gold
New Paltz, New York
November 2016

Contents

Introduction

Welcome to a neglected yet important topic—dining manners. It is an area that scares many people unnecessarily and makes them anxious when, in fact, manners are designed to help people enjoy dinner parties, special events, and other situations where other people are involved and should be considered. Originally, advice about manners was provided to ensure that everyone understood his role and expectations at formal dinners when staff were responsible for setting the table, preparing the food, serving the food, and cleaning up. However, the world has changed, and advice about manners has changed as well. Since it is still true that bad manners and bad habits make other people uncomfortable, it is important to learn good manners so that you can enjoy yourself and the company of others.

There are lots of books about manners, but most of them are full of rules and contain little in the way of explanation as to why these common practices have become widely accepted. Precious few describe good and bad manners together. This book contains 165 photographs of good and bad manners as well as explanations of what makes them so. These images will help you understand, in a fun and humorous way, the practice of good manners.

Who Will Benefit from This Book?

Modern American Manners has been written primarily for students entering the workplace, domestic and international business professionals who need to know appropriate manners, and anyone, young or old, interested in both good and bad table manners. It covers a range of personal and business situations, providing advice for everyone as well as professionals, business owners and managers, students, visitors to the United States, and others who may not have learned about good manners at home. For international business people and students who want to learn the way of doing things in the United States, this book will be especially useful. In addition, it has been written for anyone who is interested in teaching good table manners to their family members, including their children; in pointing out good practices of table manners to friends or colleagues; and in seeking advice for themselves for situations in which they may not be sure what is proper etiquette.

People who did not grow up eating meals at the dinner table with parents, aunts and uncles, and grandparents will find help in these pages. They often did not learn proper behavior at the dinner table and may want to fill this gap in their education. Others find that their careers and opportunities for professional advancement have been hampered, if not destroyed, by their lack of proper—or appropriate—table manners, and they want to remove this obstacle to their professional development and interaction with colleagues. Others like to dine in restaurants and want to be more comfortable in situations where they find themselves without guiding principles to decide what is appropriate and what is not. Hopefully, this book will contribute to making all dining events more pleasant and anxiety-free for everyone.

This book is written in the second person point of view, in conversation with you, the reader, to make it more approachable and easy to read. Although it would be more accurate to refer to both "hosts" and "hostesses" to avoid making sexist assumptions about entertaining and to acknowledge the fact that it is increasingly common to find only one host or hostess or two hosts and two hostesses, we use the word "host" to refer to both hosts and hostesses for the sake of clarity. The one area where "hostess" is used, however, is in the section on hostess gifts because the term "hostess gifts" has become the normal phrase to refer to gifts to the person or the people entertaining you.

Global and Local Manners

While this book is designed to provide you, whether host or guest, with information about what to do and when to do it at a dinner party, it can be applied to many other situations. The focus of this book is on manners in the United States. In other countries, different habits and traditions follow other principles for good manners and other ways of doing things. For example, in Korea and China, diners expect to use toothpicks at the end of a meal to clean food from their teeth (while covering their mouths with their hands or a napkin), and a container of wrapped or unwrapped toothpicks is typically placed on the table. However, that practice would be unusual and make some people uncomfortable in the United States, where people tend to use toothpicks away from the table. In some countries, making noise while eating is encouraged as a signal that you are enjoying the meal. In the United States, it is strongly discouraged.

In some parts of the United States, there are regional and ethnic differences about various aspects of dinner parties. This book does not address those local idiosyncrasies, since general good manners are applicable in most situations—business, professional, and social. Our goal is to encourage you to learn and practice good manners so that you can enjoy the pleasures of eating meals with business and professional colleagues, with friends, and with family members while not embarrassing yourself. Bad manners can be detrimental to your enjoyment, your friendships, and your career. Whatever you adapt from these ideas and make work in your own groups, we celebrate.

Scope of This Book

While this book focuses on table manners—at-home dinner parties, restaurant dinners, business events, and other special situations such as cocktail parties—it is not a complete guide to all the situations that require proper manners in life. That would take an encyclopedia. (However, the bibliography contains a wide range of suggestions for those who want more extensive information.)

In addition, this book cannot and does not address all the possible dining situations. For example, it is not about weddings, backyard barbecues, or special ethnic parties. It also does not cover extremely formal events such as meeting royalty, attending state dinners, or participating in an event at the White House or other residences of heads of state. However, some of the basic principles apply in all those situations; there is just more protocol and formal etiquette involved. (For a discussion of protocol, etiquette, and manners, see **Chapter 1. Civility, Manners, and Etiquette**.)

Since most people do not hire or employ other people to cook and serve dinner parties, this book was written for those who entertain without the assistance of professional help, or who entertain in restaurants. It provides almost no advice about managing caterers or employees hired for the evening. However, the principles of good table manners work in almost all situations and are, therefore, applicable to dinner parties staffed by professionals.

Ways to Use this Book

This book contains photographs that illustrate what to do and what not to do, according to commonly accepted contemporary standards. The writing provides explanations and advice that are supplemented by the images, some of which you may recognize from your experience, and some you may not be able to imagine anyone doing. If these not-to-do situations are new to you, congratulate yourself on how much you know about manners. They can still be fun to look at and show to others.

The book can be read in any order, reviewed as a reference, or shown to others to provide advice. The Table of Contents provides detailed information about what each chapter includes, and the pictures provide images of various aspects of both bad and good manners. We recommend reading the entire book; however, there are ways to read for specific purposes.

If you are going to be a guest at a dinner party and are not sure how to behave, read:
- **Chapter 2. Conduct Becoming a Guest**
- **Chapter 5. Cocktail Party Manners**
- **Chapter 7. Pet Peeves at Dinner Parties**
- **Chapter 9. Enjoying Yourself**

If you are planning to host a party, consider reading:
- **Chapter 3. Conduct Becoming a Host**
- **Chapter 4. A Well-Set Table**
- **Chapter 7. Pet Peeves at Dinner Parties**
- **Chapter 8. Special Situations: Political Events, Dating Manners, and Very Formal Settings**
- **Chapter 9. Enjoying Yourself**

If you are going to be involved in a business event, read:
- **Chapter 1. Civility, Manners, and Etiquette**
- **Chapter 2. Conduct Becoming a Guest**
- **Chapter 5. Cocktail Party Manners**
- **Chapter 6. Manners in Business Settings**
- **Chapter 7. Pet Peeves at Dinner Parties**

- **Chapter 8. Special Situations: Political Events, Dating Manners, and Very Formal Settings**
- **Chapter 9. Enjoying Yourself**

If you are interested in table manners as a topic of amusement, read:
- **Chapter 1. Civility, Manners, and Etiquette**
- **Chapter 4. A Well-Set Table**
- **Chapter 5. Cocktail Party Manners**
- **Chapter 6. Manners in Business Settings**
- **Chapter 7. Pet Peeves at Dinner Parties**
- **Chapter 8. Special Situations: Political Events, Dating Manners, and Very Formal Settings**

You may find that the photographs trigger an interest in various topics and compel you to read that section or chapter. Look at the chapter from the perspective of the pictures, and you will find it easy and fun to read while you are learning at the same time.

If you want to read more, you will find a bibliography of works cited at the end of the book. Along with providing more etiquette information, these references also illustrate the range of opinions about some aspects of manners.

Learning about and practicing proper manners will help you enjoy the pleasures of sharing good food, good wine, and good company. It is a joy in life to sit at the table and engage in lively, interesting, intelligent, and important conversation with family, friends, and colleagues. As Craig Claiborne, food critic of the *New York Times* for many years and a bon vivant, wrote, "Even more so than the evening's tangible ingredients—the food, the wine, the setting—good talk is what makes an occasion interesting and exciting."

We hope that this book will encourage you to take the time to enjoy these aspects of life, to make new friends, and to deepen your connections with your business colleagues, current friends, and family by enjoying meals together.

CHAPTER 1

Civility, Manners, and Etiquette

"Bad manners will always be frowned on and good manners admired."
—Nicholas Clayton, a professional English butler

Before we can address good and bad manners (or, in fact, anything about manners at all), we need to understand civility and graciousness—two of the fundamental issues behind manners. And once we know more about civility and graciousness, we can distinguish between manners and etiquette and learn the challenges and importance of making manners a daily habit.

Civility

What happened to civility—the way we treat one another in social situations? We used to respect individuals—whether strangers, colleagues, or friends—and treat them with politeness and cordiality even if we disagreed with them. We used to extend ourselves easily to strangers and welcome them into our lives. While we used to treat each person we met with respect, in recent times, we have dropped the decent regard that most people associate with civility. We have lost the friendly greeting, the natural smile, and the kindness that people used to extend easily to others. We no longer practice patience with other people, listen to them before speaking, or care about their opinions.

In fact, 63 percent of Americans surveyed by Powell Tate, a research firm, stated that the United States has a significant civility problem, and 71 percent said it was worse than it was several years ago. You can see the lack of consideration in daily interactions and the surprise many individuals demonstrate when confronted with a smile or a kind "hello."

Civility includes a number of behaviors that we used to take for granted. Using polite language whenever there is a choice. Smiling—rather than frowning—at people we pass on the street or meet. Letting other people complete their sentences before jumping into the conversation. All of these examples are ways we can treat other people with dignity and civility.

Civility is the opposite of self-oriented behavior, which has become more common and valued. Some commentators blame the lack of civility on the prevalence of social media and the lack of direct personal interaction, while others ascribe it to a dearth of parents teaching basic social niceties to their children. Some even blame the lack of interpersonal skills on the prevalence of games and electronic methods of communication. Whatever the cause, the lack of civility has changed the patterns of interpersonal communication and the value of kindness, generosity, and graciousness. Against this background, it becomes ever more critical to remember to practice graciousness and to demonstrate care for the other person's comfort and enjoyment in social settings.

Graciousness

While civility is a basic human regard, graciousness is a continuing and consistent perspective of thinking positively about the other person and acting accordingly. Graciousness is a way of being in the world—it is an approach to people based on kindness, consideration, and empathy. It comes from a position of caring about other people and responding to them with sensitivity and thoughtfulness. Gracious people show kindness and attention to others because they want to and because they think it is the right thing to do; they do not operate out of kindness in order to obtain some advantage. It is an other-person-oriented approach—rather than a self-oriented perspective—to interpersonal situations and life.

Gracious people are generous with their time and their spirit. They care about the other person and demonstrate that caring in a myriad of ways. They listen to the other person, demonstrate real interest in what they have to say, and ask questions to learn more. They show others little kindnesses and contribute to making the other person's life easier and better. If the person is experiencing some awkwardness or difficulty, gracious people help with the situation gently. They want the other person to be happy and to enjoy an event; they do not like watching the other person's unhappiness, awkwardness, or embarrassment.

Make people feel comfortable

Graciousness goes beyond civility and focuses on making people comfortable. In social and business situations, gracious people encourage introductions, help make connections between people, ensure that no one is left out of a discussion or a group, and bolster the confidence of those who are ill at ease.

If you have the instinct for civility and the inclination toward graciousness, you can understand manners easily and you will be able to demonstrate good manners in any situation. Gracious people know good manners and demonstrate them since they already are focused on the comfort of others.

Help individuals to their chairs

Manners

As the term is most commonly used, "manners" refers to proper and appropriate behavior in a range of social contexts. A person with good manners is a person who knows how to act, with ease, in many different situations while making other people feel comfortable and relaxed. People who possess good manners recognize the importance of making people around them feel like they belong in a social situation and that they are welcomed in the circumstances. Good manners mean valuing the quality of interpersonal experiences such as sharing a drink, a dinner, or an evening. Part of good manners involves being appropriate and gracious in any and all settings.

Although good manners often refer to the proper ways of behaving in a dining or entertaining situation, they don't have to be complicated and confusing. Perhaps one of the best definitions of manners comes from Craig Claiborne, who said, "Good manners are nothing more than common sense and consideration for others." However, common sense is not very common anymore.

Manners can be hard to define, but most of us can recognize bad manners and may want to criticize people who demonstrate them. Don't. It shows a lack of graciousness, which is a sign of poor manners. People with good manners do not want others to be uncomfortable; criticizing someone for doing something wrong only makes a difficult situation worse. Using proper manners means overlooking simple gaffes.

Having good manners means not drawing attention to the poor manners of others; it means acting kindly when others do not know what they are supposed to do or how they are supposed to do it. There are many stories of elegant hosts drinking the water in their finger bowls when they see a guest do it simply in order to make the guests comfortable. Their ability to overlook this breach of good manners is a matter of style and grace.

Do not dominate conversation or invade another person's space

Do not dominate the conversation by talking loud and not listening

How do you identify good manners? Good manners include the cordial attitude and approach that people bring to interacting with others. Being welcoming, friendly, and gracious is part of good manners. Remembering to treat other people decently and communicate with some sensitivity is part of good manners. As Emily Post has written, "Hello," "please," "thank you," "you are welcome," "I am sorry," and "good-bye" are considered essential elements of basic manners. In the United States, these phrases are used—with some variations—to communicate an appreciation for the other person. They are used to grease or lubricate interpersonal communication and exchanges. Without them, we would often seem rude or neglectful of the other person. In fact, Emily Post, a powerful arbiter of manners and etiquette, has indicated that manners are based on respect, consideration, and honesty.

Manners do not change from situation to situation. In fact, good manners belong as much at family meals as they do in restaurant settings; they matter as much in casual settings as they do at fancy events. In dining situations, good manners are one way to make sure the event goes smoothly and that everyone has a good time. As Nicholas Clayton, a professional butler, wrote, "Eating is as fundamental as breathing. It is very important, however, to learn good manners, as they help to smooth our way in the company of others. A society devoid of manners would be a jagged and jarring society of clumsiness and unfriendly behavior." Good table manners make interacting with other people much easier and provide maximum comfort for everyone involved. Manners help us enjoy dining together. Emily Post once wrote, "All the rules of table manners are made to avoid ugliness. To let anyone see what you have in your mouth is repulsive; to make a noise is to suggest an animal; to make a mess is disgusting." Most importantly, paying attention to good manners helps everyone enjoy the pleasures of good food, good drink, and good company.

Manners always make an impression on others, especially when dining. You remember a person with excellent manners, and you will not forget a person with atrocious manners. It therefore behooves all of us to learn, practice, and use excellent manners in every situation. Both good and bad manners communicate a great deal about a person.

When in doubt, use better manners than the situation warrants, since you can always simplify your behavior, but it is hard to recover from a situation where you did not show your skills.

In fact, having no decent table manners has become a deal-breaker in a job interview. It is also a deal-breaker in dating, since it often shows a disregard for the other person or a lack of willingness or ability to act graciously and comfortably in social situations where the goal is everyone's enjoyment.

Manners can, and often do, change and adapt to the times, since they depend on paying attention to the people you are with and the way your host has planned the meal.

Etiquette

While the subject of manners is about helping others feel comfortable and at ease, etiquette refers to the set of rules for what is proper in situations ranging from letter writing to extravagant weddings to simple dinner parties. The basic rules of etiquette make social situations more comfortable for everyone present.

Some of the rules of dining etiquette in the United States include:

- When asked to pass the salt or the pepper, always pass them together.
- When you want something at the table, ask for it—don't reach for it.
- When passing dishes, offer them to other people first before helping yourself.
- Do not help yourself to food served family style by using a fork or spoon that has already been in your mouth.
- Do not use your hands to eat food.
- Do not help yourself to food on another person's plate.

- Do not talk with your mouth full.

When you finish your meal, place the fork and knife or fork and spoon at four o'clock

Do not apply makeup at the table

Keep in mind, though, that rules of etiquette are not helpful if they're not accompanied by good manners. As etiquette guru Amy Vanderbilt has explained:

I believe that knowledge of the rules of living in our society makes us more comfortable even though our particular circumstances may permit us to elude them somewhat. Some of the rudest and most objectionable people I have ever known have been technically the most "correct." Some of the warmest, most loveable, have had little more than an innate feeling of what is right toward others. But, at the same time, they have had the intelligence to inform themselves, as necessary, on the rules of social intercourse as related to their own experiences. Only a great fool or a great genius is likely to flout all social grace with impunity, and neither one, doing so, makes the most comfortable companion.

In many situations, being friendly and making others comfortable are more important than knowing the rules of etiquette but refusing to act positively or graciously with other people.

"Etiquette" refers to rules for situations, and "manners" refers to habits of behavior. Etiquette refers to how to do something appropriately, and manners are a matter of not noticing if someone did it well or poorly. Manners and graciousness are about helping people be comfortable. Etiquette is about knowing the rules and the protocol and following them absolutely correctly.

Etiquette is important because the rules help everyone know what to do so that they can focus on the meal and the interaction. It has been defined as "the science of social living which consists of rules and guidelines to help social interaction run smoothly; it helps us to know how to behave and what behavior to expect from others." Others have defined it as "a set of rules and guidelines that make your personal and professional relationships more harmonious, productive, and meaningful."

While etiquette used to be limited to elegant and formal settings and entertaining primarily, it currently covers proper behavior in informal situations as well. Increasingly, etiquette is applied to a range of situations such as office etiquette, social etiquette, social media etiquette, dating etiquette, and interview etiquette. The field of etiquette also refers to matters of protocol, which covers rules that honor differences in status or position. Protocol is a matter of deference and is always appropriate, although more often an issue for diplomatic situations and parties involving senior executives or politicians. For example, protocol refers to not making a toast at a formal dinner party before the host has made his or her toast and invited others to make their toasts.

Finally, the rules of etiquette do not change. They are fixed and focus on doing the right thing in the right way.

With your new expertise in civility, graciousness, manners, and etiquette, you have the context to read the following pages.

CHAPTER 2

Conduct Becoming a Guest

"There is nothing more off-putting than sitting at the same dining table with someone with appalling table manners—you know the sort of thing: eating with the mouth open (doing an impression of a cement mixer); making dog-like slurping noises; talking and gesticulating while eating; gulping at drinks and burping; constantly scraping knife over fork to remove an abnormal amount of food build-up; resting elbows on the table with knife and fork stuck up like oars; holding the knife poised as if ready to sign a cheque; elbows stuck so far out as to resemble a black London taxi with both doors open; hunching over the plate, guarding it from some unseen predator, and shoveling in huge mouthfuls as if the food is just about to be taken away. Not a pretty picture, is it?"

—Nicholas Clayton, a professional English butler

Enjoy being invited to a dinner party

Basic table manners are a critical part of being a happy guest and one who will be invited back. They provide the guidelines to help you relax and enjoy the meal, the company, and the entire evening; focus on interesting conversation; and experience the quality of the event. Dinner parties are a time for engaging with others in good conversation, networking, and the enjoyment of good food and drink.

A well-mannered guest follows the lead of the host and enjoys himself during the event. With these two ideas in mind, you will have a great time and contribute significantly to the success of the evening.

Basic Principles of Good Manners

While you may find yourself in lots of different situations as a guest, there are five key principles of good manners that will help you in all of them. Taken together, they GRACE your behavior in any event where you are a guest.

- **G**ather clues about what to do from your host. Wait for your host to start eating, watch what they do and how they do it, and follow his lead.
- **R**efrain from dominating the conversation, eating too much, or drinking too much, all of which make other people uncomfortable and can ruin the evening.
- **A**ssist the host in making the evening a success. That can mean contributing to the conversation, assisting in serving or clearing the table if the dinner is relatively informal, and helping in whatever way you can.

- **C**are about the comfort of your fellow diners. Make good conversation by asking questions and listening well, monitor what they need to enjoy the dinner, include new people in conversations, and offer to pass items before being asked.
- **E**njoy and appreciate the food, beverages, decorations, and company. Enjoy yourself, and you will help other people enjoy themselves as well. Don't forget to show your appreciation for the evening.

These five principles will help you enjoy dinner parties and other occasions; Peter Rossi has written, "the most important thing to remember about table manners is to behave graciously. Evening at the table should be enjoying both the meal and the company, not evaluating and judging each diner's familiarity with the rules of etiquette." Good manners begin the moment in which you receive an invitation to a dinner party.

Responding to an Invitation

Most often people are invited to dinner parties and other events with a phone call, a personal conversation, or an email, so you can respond when invited, whether over the phone, in person, or by hitting "reply." However, when you are invited to a special event, such as a birthday party, an anniversary, a business function, or a celebration event, you may find the terms *RSVP* or *Regrets Only* on the hand-written note or printed invitation. In that case, you should respond promptly—and certainly by the "respond by" date—since the host needs to know how many people will be attending. It makes a big difference in planning and working with a caterer or venue in the case of a large party, and your failure to respond could be costly to the host. It is also a way to demonstrate that you are sensitive to the host's needs. In fact, responding promptly to any invitation is good manners; it shows you are not holding out for the best invitation, but responding to the first one received. The normal range of time for you to respond to a formal invitation ranges from quickly (Craig Claiborne's recommendation) to three days (Kate Spade's recommendation). Of course, if you are being invited by email and the event is only a short time away, you should respond as soon as you can.

If there is insufficient information on the invitation, feel free to inquire—by telephone, email, texting, or a note—so that you are sure about the date, time, location, dress code, and any special information. Particularly ask if you have questions about what you should wear; if you do not know what to wear, ask the host, to save you an awkward or embarrassing moment.

If the invitation is formal, it is appropriate to send a note in response. If it is informal, you have more choices about how to respond. An informal note, a phone call, or an email is appropriate. Remember, however, that if you say yes to an invitation, you should plan to be there and start to consider what kind of hostess gift would be appropriate and welcomed. Not showing up and not explaining your absence constitutes rude manners.

It is not appropriate, however, to call or email the host to find out who is coming or what is being served in order to make a decision about attending or not. Behaving in this manner is pretentious and rude. It indicates that you are hoping for a better offer or that you are not sure the host is making a dinner party good enough for you. If you are not sure you want to go, then simply decline the invitation and do so promptly so that the host can invite other people to make the party a success. Most often, the guest list has been put together with some care about who will enjoy one another and how well the guests will enjoy the evening. Often, hosts take account of dietary limitations—if they know them—and invite people with similar dietary restrictions, or at least provide a meal that each guest can eat. If you have some dietary restrictions, it is very appropriate to provide that information to the host—when you accept, with pleasure, the invitation. It helps the host with menu decisions.

If you have accepted an invitation to a dinner party and you start to get sick, you have a choice of how to proceed. It depends on how you feel and how contagious you are. On the one hand, you do not want to disappoint a host at the last minute; on the other hand, you don't want to get people sick by attending the dinner party. A simple cold that is not contagious and that can be treated with over-the-counter medication is not necessarily a reason to drop out of a party. However, a serious cold, flu, or other sickness should prompt you to alert the host that you may not be able to attend the party as planned—and you should share that information as soon as you are aware of it. That way, the host can add others to the party. A second option is to inform your host of your condition and ask him what he would like you to do—attend, stay home, or wait and see how you feel a day before the dinner party. In any case, communicating with the host is the most important action to take.

Arrive on time. Most people plan to arrive on time or within fifteen minutes of the beginning of the event—often considered being fashionably late. As Jeremiah Towers, famous restaurateur, has written, "There is no such thing as being fashionably early. Nothing puts a host off his stride more than an early guest." Although there are regional and cultural differences about arriving on time (in Canada, for example, arriving fashionably late is expected, as it is in some urban areas in the United States), you should plan to arrive at a dinner party at the time for which you are invited. (Cocktail parties are different; guests are expected to arrive during a window that extends from the time the event starts to a half hour later. See **Chapter 5. Cocktail Party Manners**.) If extenuating circumstances affect your arrival time—something you did not plan for and that causes delay—you should call the host and inform him that you expect to arrive late. If you arrive later than 15 minutes, you owe the host an apology and an explanation.

Consider several options for hostess gifts

Hostess Gifts

One of the most commonly asked questions about being a guest is: What should I bring to the hostess? Although it used to be unclear what to do, there is an increasing number of options, all of them good. Remember that the first consideration is thinking about your hostess. (Since these gifts are typically referred to as hostess gifts, the language in this section will refer exclusively to hostess regardless of whether the gifts are presented to a man or a woman.)

What does the hostess like? What would make her smile? What is appropriate for the occasion or situation? If you are invited for an informal dinner party, a simple present is appropriate. If you are invited for a very formal event or a weekend, you need to select something fancier or more valuable. For an informal dinner party, some of the most common hostess gifts include:

- A bottle of wine, champagne, artisan beer, liquor, or liqueur, depending on the preferences of the hostess. A great way to present the gift is to wrap it in a new kitchen towel and place a bow around it. Everyone needs new kitchen towels, and it becomes a reminder of the gift. It also indicates that you have thought about the gift before you left the house. At a minimum, present the bottle of wine in a brown bag or a silver bag that the liquor store provides. When you bring this gift, do not expect that it will be opened that evening for the dinner party. It is, after all, a gift for the hostess and something to be consumed at another time.

- Wine decanter. With or without a bottle of wine, a wine decanter can be a thoughtful gift for hostesses who appreciate wine and serve it at dinner parties. Small decanters can serve two people and larger ones hold a full bottle. Either two small ones or a large one, carefully wrapped, can make a special gift.

- Extra virgin olive oil. This present can solve the problem about what to do for people who do not drink or when you do not want to bring liquor. You can find an increasing number of interesting EVOs (extra virgin olive oils), often with distinctive flavors. Bringing olive oil is a gourmet compliment to the hostess.

- Vinegars that you have made—or found at a local farmer's market—that have intriguing flavors. This present is also a great compliment to the chef who appreciates extra cooking items. Special sauces also make great presents. Alternatively, you can bring an oil-and-vinegar combination.

- A box of chocolates. Chocolates are always appreciated, unless the hostess is diabetic or on a diet, and you'll find a wide range of chocolatiers and packages. These days the boxes are beautifully designed, and you can choose from truffles, milk chocolate candies, dark chocolates, and combinations.

- A bar accessory—a corkscrew, mixing pitcher, shaker, or aerator. Although unusual, these gifts can be useful, especially if you know the hostess and are aware of what she does or does not have. It shows thoughtfulness.
- Dinner napkins. A set of four or six makes a lovely present, and most people can use another set of cloth napkins. If you know the colors of the tablecloths used or the colors of the dining room, bringing dinner napkins that match or complement the colors is a very thoughtful way to show you appreciate the invitation.
- Cocktail napkins, particularly if they come in an interesting pattern or set of colors that match the colors in the living room or if they have intriguing images or sayings.
- Coasters. Hostesses can always use more, or new, coasters to hold drinks and protect their tables. They can be paper, cardboard, cork, wood, or stone. Often, souvenir coasters with pictures or images of special locations can make a very thoughtful gift.
- A small cheese board with some cheese. A small cheese board is a thoughtful gift and one that many people do not own or think to give. Add a piece of cheese that you like or that you know your hostess has not tried, and you have a wonderful present. A small package of special crackers makes a great addition to the cheese and the small cheese board. Alternatively, cheese, crackers, and a special cheese knife make an excellent hostess present. You'll find small cheese boards and interesting cheese knives at craft fairs and in artisan shops.
- Fresh vegetables. Depending on the season and your knowledge of the hostess, a selection of fresh vegetables can be an unusual and highly appreciated hostess gift. If your hostess likes to cook, the freshest vegetable from a farmer's market or your garden can be a wonderful addition to what she has in her house. However, if you know the hostess is going away, these vegetables can be an unwelcome burden.
- A pound of special coffee with a measuring spoon or coffee ladle. If you know that your hostess likes coffee, an unusual flavor or special artisan coffee—especially in the form of beans, since they last longer than ground coffee—can make a very nice present. Combining it with one or two handmade coffee mugs or travel mugs makes an even nicer present.

- A package or packages of special teas. One way to show that you know your hostess well is to provide her with a special pound of loose tea or a set of tea bags that appeal to her taste. Sharing special teas that you have found can be a real treat. Add a mug or two or a small teapot to give the gift even more flair.
- Hand-woven baskets. Most people appreciate decorative hand-woven baskets. They can be filled with food, dried flowers, cocktail napkins, jams and preserves, or just given alone.
- Box of soap. Some people appreciate specialty soaps, handmade soaps, scented soaps, and intriguing shapes of soaps. Soap is a present that is clearly intended for the hostess to enjoy and not share with the dinner guests.
- Hand towels. These cloth—or paper—towels can be a thoughtful gift because many hostesses provide them in the powder room or guest bathroom and can never have too many. Bringing towels that match the décor or color scheme of the powder room shows that you thought about what to bring and spent the time to find the right present.
- A small plant in a planter. The colorful and long-lasting value of a plant makes it a great present because it does not require any attention from the hostess, when you arrive. If you know the house and how much light there is, you can bring a plant that is more likely to thrive in that environment. Alternatively, your hostess might appreciate a larger plant that can be placed on a deck or porch.
- A book. If you know the person well enough to purchase a book, or if you find a new book on food or entertaining, it can make a welcome present. Many hostesses receive bottles of wine, flowers, and other gifts; a book can be a new delight.
- Jellies, jams, preserves, or condiments—especially if you have made them. These homemade gifts are unusual and often have special meaning and flavors.

You can prepare yourself for being a guest by purchasing multiple sets of interesting napkins, coasters, cheese boards, and other nonperishable items whenever you see them. You will then be prepared for any occasion that calls for a hostess present.

Gifts you do not want to bring include food for use that evening (unless asked), cut flowers, or something ostentatious. Food is inappropriate because the hostess has already developed the menu and prepared the meal and will now feel required to add your dish, which may or may not complement the rest of the meal. If you have arranged to bring a dish ahead of time, bring the dish and all the condiments, platters or bowls, and serving utensils you will need. You don't want to interrupt the hostess to ask for vinegar, grated cheese, a knife and cutting board, or space in the oven to finish the dish you brought. It disrupts the kitchen, provides a challenge for the hostess to be gracious while doing the rest of the meal, and may take up precious space in the kitchen. Prepare your dish thoroughly ahead of time and bring everything you need—do not depend on the hostess for anything.

Cut flowers are awkward and thoughtless because they require the hostess to find a vase, put them in water, arrange them, and decide where to place them in the house, all of which detracts from her ability to host and greet other guests. In addition, it is presumptuous of you to assume what kind of flowers would look good in her home. Your sense of what is tasteful may differ radically from the hostess's opinion. Arranged flowers in a vase or container, however, can be a lovely present that does not require arranging and disrupting the plans for entertaining. Make sure that they are arranged carefully so that they travel well—or that you can protect them during travel to the hostess's home. It would be awkward to arrive with a wet mess of flowers.

The reason for avoiding ostentatious gifts is to prevent awkwardness for the hostess, who must accept something way beyond the level of the meal or the event. A big gift says more about your need to show off or intimidate others than your appreciation for the invitation or the work involved in hosting. And it often creates a difficult scene. Being invited for a simple dinner on the deck and bringing—unasked—a case of wine shows a complete lack of understanding of the event. A bottle of wine, or two, would be sufficient. On the other hand, if you are invited to a formal dinner party and you bring one small package of cocktail napkins, you are not demonstrating an awareness of the planning and work involved in throwing the party.

If you are not able to bring a hostess present or do not want to, you can always send something later; however, most hostesses appreciate a gift at the time you arrive. It is the thoughtfulness that counts. (For more information, see **Thank You Notes** and **Thank You Presents** later in this chapter.) And you should never feel forced to bring a present. As Craig Claiborne said, "The truth is that a guest never really has to bring anything at all, except his own good cheer." And coming to a dinner party in a good mood, ready to enjoy yourself and appreciate the other guests, is a great contribution to the success of the evening.

Greet the host or hostess in a friendly manner

Greetings

One of the first events of any dinner party is greeting the host and then the other guests. The greeting should be genuine and open. If you know the host, then you know what to say when you arrive, and you probably know what to expect as well. If the host is new to you, extend your hand and introduce yourself while thanking him for inviting you.

When escorted into the living room—or the location where the drinks are being served—enter the room with a smile, regardless of how you feel, and be prepared to introduce yourself to as many people as you can without touring the room. It is your chance to meet and get to know the people who are here for the event. In a small, informal dinner party, you may be sitting down with drinks. In a large dinner event or buffet, cocktails may be a stand-up affair, and you will be expected to mingle and meet the other guests. (For more information about what to do at cocktail parties, see **Chapter 5. Cocktail Party Manners**.)

Even if you do not feel like an extrovert, this cocktail period is the time for you to put on your best face and start interesting conversations. One way to start this process—especially if you are uncomfortable going up to strangers—is to consider yourself the host and introduce yourself to everyone. This activity will become easier as you move around the room and introduce yourself because most people are also often uncomfortable at this point. Making them comfortable can also make you more comfortable. Talking to them may reduce their discomfort and contribute to their and your relaxation. If you are open to it, you will probably get to know the people involved and find someone who is really interesting.

The cocktail period is also an opportunity to learn people's names—or relearn them, if you have forgotten them. You can always say, "You look very familiar, but I cannot come up with your name right now." Most people will reintroduce themselves. Whenever you have a chance to introduce people to each other, make sure you provide their names and something about them. It facilitates the conversation immensely. After all, the purpose of the cocktail part of the evening is to mix and mingle and meet the other people—or reconnect and catch up if you know them all—before sitting down to dinner.

Enjoy cocktails before dinner

Cocktails or Before-Dinner Drinks

When the host offers you a drink, accept it graciously or ask for something nonalcoholic if you are not drinking. You do not need to indulge in a long explanation, but do not accept alcohol if it is not right for you! Most hosts have no difficulty with that situation. What is hard for them is seeing you without a drink in your hand. Therefore, accept something or go to the bar area and pour yourself a nonalcoholic beverage and join in the party.

When offered a cocktail or drink before dinner, feel free to ask, "What are you serving?" and decide among the choices. If the choices do not include something you want or are comfortable drinking, simply request a glass of sparkling or still water. If the host has a full bar, you can ask for what you want. But do not expect the host to make you anything you request. Asking for an obscure cocktail or a specialty drink can make the host uncomfortable and often draws him away from his guests. Don't be surprised if he indicates the bar and suggests you make your own drink!

Part of the value of cocktails before dinner is a chance to get to know the guests and establish new connections. Therefore, make sure that you engage each person you meet in conversation. Ask them about aspects of their lives or current activities so that you can find something to discuss. Ask about books, plays, concerts, and community events.

The more people you meet, the more comfortable you and the rest of the guests will become. In fact, you share with the host the responsibility for making the evening successful. The best way, according to Arthur Inch, a proper English butler, is to "make every effort to meet people you don't already know. Husbands and wives should mingle, not huddle together, excluding others."

Use the time during cocktails to remember the names of the guests and practice pronouncing them correctly. Using their names when first introduced, as well as associating them with some activity they do or story they tell, will help you remember them.

During the cocktail hour, help yourself to the hors d'oeuvres and other foods put out for your pleasure using the cocktail napkins as needed. Remember, however, not to eat too much before the meal, because dinner will be served. When called to dinner, respond promptly to the invitation to come to the dining room and leave your drink glass behind. You will find new glasses—appropriate for the dinner—on the table. Sometimes, the host will request you bring your wine glasses to the table. In that case, please do.

Sitting Down to Eat

If you are attending a simple dinner party, wait for a cue about where to sit. Often, the host will invite individuals to sit where they are comfortable, but others have a clear idea of who should sit with whom and have organized the table. You may see place cards, but informal dinner parties often dispense with these niceties, so you may have no formal cue about where you are supposed to sit.

Sit where the host asks you to sit

In this case, ask the host where he wants to place you. Typically, a host sits at a particular place, and the rest of the party is arrayed accordingly. Sometimes, he will take his seat or at least stand behind his chair and then explain where others should sit. The guest of honor—if there is one—is seated at the right of the host since most people are right-handed, and the rest of the guests are placed around the table according to the host's plans.

Traditionally, dinner party seating is arranged according to the principle of alternating men and women (where possible) and separating partners and spouses. This practice encourages interaction among people who do not normally dine together.

This waiting point for the host to indicate where you should sit is a great opportunity to show your graciousness. You can ask if you can help the host bring dishes to the table. He may appreciate the help, but he may not. Remember GRACE and offer to assist, but do not continue to offer if he declines your help. Sometimes guests make it harder on a host who knows what he wants to do and how to do it. Stopping to explain may take more time than he wants to devote to the task. When everyone is seated, it is time to begin the meal.

Beginning the Meal

When you sit down at the table, the first thing to do is to take your napkin, unfold it, and place it in your lap. It indicates that you are prepared for the meal, ready to participate, and eager to enjoy the evening. It also shows respect toward the host and demonstrates your good manners. In some situations, the host will say grace—or a nondenominational prayer—or invite a particular individual to say grace over the meal. If there is a minister, priest, rabbi, imam, or other religious figure at the table, that individual might expect to be requested to say grace. In that case, simply bow your head and listen to what is said, regardless of your religious or spiritual inclination. Alternative forms of grace include a quiet moment before the meal or a ritual of holding hands and saying, "May we all meet again around this festive board."

Say grace if invited

Once the grace has been said, you can begin the conversation or continue a previous conversation, but do not begin to eat until everyone is served and the host either begins to eat or puts his flatware on the plate, the universal cue to begin eating.

Take the butter and move it to your bread and butter plate

Bread and Butter

One of the first items many people eat—especially in restaurants—is bread or rolls. The proper way to eat bread or rolls and butter or oil is to take a roll or slice of bread from a central basket (unless it is served to you or passed to you) and place it on your bread and butter plate, which is located to the left of the dinner plate. If using butter, take some from a serving dish for the butter using the utensil provided with the butter serving dish and place it on the bread and butter plate. Break the bread or roll into a bite-sized piece, then take the amount of butter you think you will need and butter the piece with your butter knife. Then you can eat the bread or roll. If you are using olive oil, pour a bit of oil onto your bread and butter plate, break off a piece of the roll or bread, dip it in the olive oil, and then enjoy it.

Do not eat a roll in one bite

Do not butter the whole roll at one time or eat the whole roll at the same time; instead, butter and eat individual portions. People with poor manners bite the bread off in their mouth and then butter the next piece. It is more sanitary to eat one piece at a time and much more pleasant to watch a person eat only a bite-sized piece of bread or roll rather than a huge mouthful. Remember to take only small mouthfuls of food at any time, since participating in the conversation at the table is an important role for you to play as a guest.

Unusual Foods

You may find yourself served food—such as artichokes, lobster, crabs, mussels, and caviar—that you have no idea how to eat. In these situations, the most appropriate action is to observe the people around you eat it. That way, you can follow their example. If it is still not clear to you, you have two other choices: ask for help, which most people are delighted to provide, or refrain from eating that item. Keep in mind that food at dinner parties will usually be prepared in a manner that makes it easy to eat. For example, hosts are more likely to serve artichoke hearts instead of the whole artichoke and lobster tails or crab rather than a full lobster or crab legs.

Carrying on Conversations

One of the major reasons to give a dinner party is the delight in having a group of people together to enjoy one another's company and to engage in interesting conversation. Therefore, one of the key rules for guests is to participate actively and appropriately in the conversation at the table. That means listening, acknowledging what people say, disagreeing politely and graciously, and presenting ideas and feelings articulately.

In large dinner parties, you should talk to the person on your left and the person on your right. It is often too difficult and very awkward to carry on a discussion across the table. Sometimes, the party is small enough to facilitate one conversation at the table. When engaging in conversations that encompass the entire table, take your cue from the host about the topic and the approach to the topic.

Feel free to contribute and make the conversation more successful, but refrain from dominating the conversation and attacking someone for his beliefs or opinions. Of course, in some circles and among some ethnic groups, the dining-room table and dinner parties are occasions for passionate, loud, and engaging conversation. In that case, join in at that level after you have determined the expectations at that table. Otherwise, you may want—or need—to modulate your volume, speed, and passion about the topics being discussed.

If you see someone who is not talking, invite that person to share her opinion or ask for a contribution to the topic. However, monitor the extent to which you are singling out this person and the individual's reaction to your invitation. Some people are delighted by an invitation to the conversation and have not figured out how to participate. Others are more comfortable listening and not participating actively—either with the topic being discussed or in general. If you think the person would be uncomfortable joining the larger conversation, start an individual conversation and make her welcome in this manner if it does not interfere with the general dinner conversation.

Watch what to do with too many glasses

Glasses and Stemware

One of the many aspects of table manners that scares some people is being presented with several glasses and not knowing what to do. A simple rule can help you out of that situation; it involves sequence and order. In a dinner party situation, where wine is being served along with the food, the glass nearest you to the right of the dinner plate is typically used for the first wine course, and the rest of the wine glasses are placed in front of you and toward the center of the table according to the order of their service. At the end of the line of glasses, you will find the water goblet. (Some hosts place the water goblet as the first glass, just above the knife and spoon. There is no required placement; the current focus on drinking lots of water encourages hosts to place that glass so that it is the easiest one to reach.)

If there is more than one wine glass, use the one closest to you first and then use them, in order, moving away from you. If you decide to skip wine for a particular course, skip that glass and use the next glass in line. Another simple trick is to observe the host in his selection of stemware for each course.

Pouring water for others at the table can also be a difficult or scary practice. In most cases, there will be a water pitcher—of glass, ceramic, or silver—on the table. Sometimes, there are bottles of mineral or flat water. If you see guests to your left or right with half-empty glasses, you should offer them some water. Pour theirs first and then yours. Follow a cardinal rule of good manners: always serve those around you before serving yourself.

When lifting a water goblet or wine glass, remember to lift it by the bowl and then hold it by the stem; if possible, lift it by the stem directly. You do not want to hold the bowl because the heat of your hand warms the water or wine.

Hold wine glasses by the stem and not the bowl

Enjoy your wine

Raise a glass to your lips for a sip of wine and then return it to the table. Holding it while gesticulating is not a good idea.

Remember to modulate your intake of beverages. No one wants to have dinner with a person who has had too much to drink and makes a fool of himself. When in doubt, drink extra water and drink much less wine than you want to.

Toast the host or the event if you wish

If you wish to make a toast—after the host has made one or, if not, after asking his permission to make a toast—call for the attention of those at the table and raise your glass, indicating that you want to make a toast. Hold your glass high to get everyone's attention. At a formal dinner party, you should stand to make a toast. The normal time to make a toast is after the host has been seated or after everyone has been seated and served the food. It can be an auspicious way to begin the dinner, and many guests make toasts thanking the host for the lovely table and meal. When you make a toast honoring the host or the guest of honor, look directly at the person to whom you are making the toast. That gesture encourages others to do so, as well, and honors the individual being toasted. It also enables everyone to recognize the person being honored by the toast.

When toasting, hold your glass above your dinner plate—but not too high—while you make the toast and then raise it higher to indicate the drinking should begin. In some situations, the host is expected to make the first toast, but it is never inappropriate to thank the host graciously with a toast to his hospitality, excellent food, wonderful wine, or superb event. Of course, do not say anything that you do not really mean. That would be worse than not making a toast at all. As Emily Post said, "Keep whatever you say short, positive and to the point—you want the spotlight to be on the toastee, not you."

If you are being toasted, do not touch your glass until the toast is over. At that point, return the toast to the person who gave it or to the group for their good wishes and the celebratory moment by tipping your glass to the person who spoke. Whatever you say, keep it short and sincere. If you are uncomfortable making a return toast, simply say, "Thank you" as a way to show your appreciation. It is inappropriate to start a thank-you toast to the person who toasted you and begin a round of clinking glasses.

Do not capture attention with a knife against your wine glass

Do not bang a knife against your wine glass before making a toast at a dinner party. Simply say you want to make a toast. Raising your glass after the short speech is the clue to others that they can sip their wine at that point. After you have made your toast—short and sweet and to the point—take a sip of your wine (or sparkling wine, sparkling cider, or sparkling water) along with the other guests and put your glass back on the table.

Toasting is an art, and if you do not feel prepared for a toast, refrain from making one. There is no need to make a toast in any situation—the major exception being weddings, when the father of the bride, the father of the groom, and the best man are expected to make formal toasts—and it is better to pass on offering a toast than to make one in which you and others will be embarrassed. Toasts are appropriate at small dinner parties and large events, but unnecessary at a modestly sized dinner party.

At large dinner parties, when it is almost impossible for each of the guests to clink their glasses together, it is very appropriate to explain the circle toast (developed originally by Robert Mondavi). For a circle toast, everyone raises their glasses while the person making the toast says what he wants to say, and then touches his glass to the glass on the right. That person then clinks the glass on her right, and the clinking goes around the table until it returns to the person making the toast. At that point—and not before—everyone raises their glasses a bit higher and takes a sip of wine (or other appropriate beverage), and the toast is concluded. The person making the toast then sits down or sits back in his chair.

Flatware

People who are unsure of their manners are also worried about how to use certain flatware—forks, knives, and spoons. They fear that they will embarrass themselves or others by using the inappropriate utensil. While a common fear, it is an easy one to overcome by remembering two critical rules:

- Watch the host or hostess
- Eat from the outside in

Watching the host means observing what flatware he is using and following that pattern. If he picks up a fork when you think you should use a spoon, you should pick up a fork and watch how he eats the dish. If he uses both a knife and fork, then you should feel free to follow that pattern. In these situations, imitation is the sincerest form of flattery, and you cannot go wrong by following the example of your host, a practice appropriate for stemware (sometimes called drinkware because many glasses do not include stems) use as well. Imitation also works well when you are not sure if the customs of your host are different from your own, especially if he was raised abroad.

If the host does not provide you with any clues about which piece of flatware to use, remember to eat from the outside in, which means that if the course calls for a fork and knife, use the fork on the furthest left and the knife at the furthest right. If it calls for a spoon, take the outside spoon. Because this rule will provide you with good guidance in most—if not all—dining situations, it is worth remembering.

Good manners require that you handle the flatware gracefully. Use your fork or spoon in your right hand to pick up food and place it in your mouth. Put only bite-sized morsels on your utensil. When cutting food, pick up your fork in your right hand, pass it to your left hand, and then turn it over so that you can use it to hold meat and other food items you need to cut. Cut the piece you want to eat, put the knife on the top edge of the plate, and transfer the fork to your right hand. Use your fork to pick up the food you want to eat and transfer it to your mouth. Your left hand should stay in your lap except when you use it to hold your fork when cutting your food. (If you are left-handed, the process is reversed.)

This American way of eating requires that you cut your meat or fish one piece at a time when at a dinner party. The way the table is set tells you that you are expected to use the American way of eating. The forks are on the left with the tines up, the knives and spoons are on the right with the bowls down. In the continental style of eating, the table is set with the tines of the forks down and the bowls of the spoons up.

In Great Britain and in some European countries, the proper way to eat is to keep the fork in the left hand, both to hold the food when cutting it and then to move the food to the mouth. The knife remains in operation, often holding the food against the fork while it moves toward the mouth. However, the knife is not raised high enough to get near or enter the mouth. In this style of eating, the knife serves two functions—to cut the food and to hold the food on the fork during eating.

If you are presented with an Asian meal and chopsticks, you are expected to use them for the meal. However, if you are not skilled in the use of chopsticks and do not want to use them, you can ask for a fork or a spoon. You may be provided with two sets of chopsticks: one to serve yourself from a series of platters and the other to use to eat food from the plate or bowl in front of you. Remember to always use the serving chopsticks—often of a different color and sometimes larger and clearly different from your personal chopsticks—to bring food to your plate, not to eat with them (for sanitary reasons, as well as good etiquette).

At most dinner parties, the table will be set with five utensils—two forks, a butter knife, a dinner knife, and a spoon—or sometimes with seven pieces. In a five-piece place setting, the fork on the far left will be for salad or an appetizer and the entrée fork will be larger and closer to the plate. If the salad is served after the main course, then the larger fork will be on the outside and the salad fork will be closer to the plate. The knife will be on the right-hand side of the plate with the blade pointed toward the plate. Beside it will be a spoon for dessert. In a seven-piece place setting, there will be two forks on the left of the plate, a butter knife on the bread and butter plate, two knives to the right of the plate, and two spoons; sometimes, there are more forks and fewer spoons. In more formal settings, the butter knife is often placed horizontally or vertically on top of the bread and butter plate. When you see three forks, it is an indication that you will have an appetizer course, a salad course, and a main course. If you see two knives, one may be for the appetizer course and the other for the main course or one for the main course and one for the salad course (since Europeans eat their salad courses with a fork and a knife). Two spoons indicate you may be having both an appetizer course and a soup course.

In some dinner parties, a fork and spoon—used for dessert—are placed horizontally above the dinner plate, since the British fashion of eating dessert using both a fork and spoon for dessert is growing in popularity in the United States. You may find these pieces of flatware placed horizontally above the dinner plate, indicating that they are saved for the dessert course. In this case, the spoon will be facing to the right and the fork to the left with the spoon above the fork. This practice allows the fork and spoon to slide down beside the dessert plate or bowl without touching the tines of the fork or the bowl of the spoon. This maintains cleanliness and food safety while providing a safe location for the dessert utensils while dinner is being eaten.

At most dinner parties, you will know how to handle the various forks, knives, and spoons as long as you observe your host. But knowing the general rules about flatware will help you relax and enjoy the meal. (For more information about other flatware, see the section on **Being Served in Very Formal Settings** in **Chapter 8. Special Situations: Political Events, Dating Manners, and Very Formal Settings**.)

Do not reach across the table

Reaching or Passing Food

One of the key aspects of good manners involves asking for things to be passed to you rather than reaching for them. If there are dishes or beverages at the table that you want, always request that someone pass the dish. Reaching raises the problem of dragging your sleeves across the table, potentially knocking over glasses or table decorations, and probably making a mess. In addition, it is awkward and clumsy—something you do not want to see at a dinner party. In some countries, such as Thailand and China, dishes are meant to be shared, and you should only help yourself to a small portion—what you can eat in a few bites—since the expectation is that people will serve themselves several times. In the United States, most people expect to take what they will eat for the meal when the dishes are being passed around the table.

In addition to the general principle of passing and not reaching, there are a few specific guidelines about passing certain items. When a person asks for the salt or the pepper, you should always pass both of them—holding them from the bottom or carefully from the sides—even if they do not want both. It provides guests with options, prevents embarrassment if you pass the wrong one, and saves another passing situation if the individual decides to use the other condiment. It is also good manners to taste your food before you salt or pepper it; otherwise, you insult the cook who has spent considerable time making a special meal.

If a person asks for sauce, mustard, cheese, relish, or another small item designed to complement the meal, pass it to them with care. Ensure that the serving spoon is firmly in the dish before passing it. If you want the condiment, and it is not located within easy reach, ask your neighbor for it. Do not reach across the table for it or ask across the table for it to be passed. If your neighbor cannot reach it, he or she should ask the next person for it. This practice helps to avoid attention to passing dishes and prevent interruptions in the dinner table conversation.

The one exception to this rule is at the beginning of the meal when everyone is passing lots of dishes and it is up to the host—with assistance from everyone at the table—to ensure that all guests have had a chance to serve themselves the dishes as well as the grated cheese, mustard, sauce, or other condiments provided. When passing all the dishes, the host will normally start passing them in a counterclockwise direction because it is more convenient for most people to hold a dish in the left hand and serve with the right hand.

Common Poor Manners and Courtesy

There are lots of errors that people make at dinner tables, and most hosts easily and graciously overlook them. The purpose of good manners is to keep the focus on the food and friendship, and not create interruptions or barriers to the enjoyment of a wonderful evening. The most common errors include the following:

- *Talking with your mouth full.* When at a dinner table, make sure that you have finished chewing and swallowing your food before speaking. If you are called on to answer a question and you have food in your mouth, raise your hand or point to your mouth to indicate that you are still chewing, and the person will be glad to wait for you. If you must speak at that moment, cover your mouth with your hand so that no one can see your mouth full of food and speak with your mouth covered. Then complete the chewing and swallowing of your food.

- *Eating with your mouth open.* Close your mouth when chewing food. No one wants to see you macerate food; it is not an appealing sight to watch someone eat and swallow. Remember to completely chew your food so you don't choke on a large piece of food; it also aids in your digestion. A good rule of thumb to follow is to chew your food a bit more than you need to so that you can swallow it easily and comfortably.

Do not chew food with your mouth open

Do not use your fingers to eat food

- *Eating with your fingers.* It is messy, awkward, and unmannerly. There are exceptions—eating an artichoke is very difficult without using your fingers—but avoid picking up chicken bones, pork chops, lamb chops, or steak bones to get the last little piece of meat. Use your knife and fork and leave what you cannot retrieve using the proper flatware.

- *Chewing gum at the table.* Don't bring gum to the table at a dinner party or even use it during the cocktail party. It is bad manners and detracts from your appearance and the enjoyment of those around you. If you chew gum to improve your breath, try a mint instead. Mints often work better and dissolve in your mouth, thereby eliminating the problem of disposing of the gum.

- *Slurping soup.* When eating soup, fill your spoon by moving it away from you in the soup bowl. In this way, you can be sure not to spill it on yourself inadvertently. It also helps you cool a hot soup a bit and make it more palatable. If you are eating a cold soup, still move the spoon away from you. When taking the soup from the spoon into your mouth, be aware of the sound(s) you make. Slurping is not a good sound to hear at a dinner table in the United States. In some other countries, it is encouraged and expected. The soup should be brought to your lips and sipped quietly. The spoon does not go all the way into your mouth.

Do not ignore your tablemates or blow your nose

- *Blowing your nose.* Do not blow your nose at the table. If you need to do so, excuse yourself and go into another room to blow your nose into your handkerchief and not into the dinner napkin. If you inadvertently left a handkerchief at home, go to the bathroom and use tissues or toilet paper, making sure to toss them in the wastebasket and wash your hands so that you do not bring your germs back to the table.

Do not pick your teeth at the table

- *Picking your teeth at the dinner table.* While it may be acceptable in some cultures, it is not standard practice in the United States and is not a behavior you should practice at a dinner party. If you are in a situation where using a toothpick is acceptable at the table, remember to cover your mouth while you do it.
- *Smoking or asking to smoke at the table.* Because so few people smoke and smoking will affect the enjoyment of the food and wine, it is not appropriate to smoke—or even to ask to smoke—at a dinner party. If you must smoke, wait until after the dinner is over and everyone is moving to the other room. That shift gives you the opportunity to slip outside and have a cigarette, cigar, or pipe. Otherwise, simply refrain until you leave the party.
- *Applying makeup or combing your hair.* These activities are best reserved for the bathroom or at least for a private location away from the table. The likelihood of scattering powder and other makeup ingredients or stray hairs on the food and the dinner table is very high and shows your lack of concern for other people at

the table. While many women increasingly apply a bit of lipstick at the end of a meal in a restaurant, they should retire to the restroom for that activity.

Do not read your tablet at the table

- *Using technology.* Cell phones and tablets do not belong at the table. They disrupt the flow of the conversation and carry a message that the individuals at the table and the party are less important than something happening elsewhere—a statement you do not want to make as a considerate guest. Therefore, leave your cell phone with your coat or turn it off at the party, unless someone asks you to research some fact. In that case, turning on the phone and looking something up can contribute to the success of the evening. However, after it is used, turn it off and put it away. In fact, some hosts collect cell phones from their guests upon arrival to prevent their use during the evening.

These examples of poor manners show the value of making everyone at the table feel comfortable. Guests will feel uncomfortable if they witness the behaviors mentioned. Therefore, always think of how your behavior will be seen and what impact it will have on others.

Do not place your elbows on the table

Fingers, Hands, and Elbows

When you are not eating during the dinner party, the best place to rest your hands is in your lap, a common habit in Europe, but less common in the United States, where many people rest their forearms on the table. Putting your hands in your lap facilitates your listening to the speaker, whether it is the person beside you or across the table, and it prevents your bumping people or dishes with your hands or arms on the table. In fact, if you are listening carefully, you should place your fork and knife—or spoon, depending on what utensil you are using at that moment and for what course—on the plate and rest your hands in your lap. Placing your hands or elbows on the table is neither sanitary nor pleasant. If you must rest something on the table, you can lean on your forearms, making sure that your elbows are not on the table in any fashion.

Besides eating, the other use for your fingers and hands can be gesturing, which is entirely appropriate so long as it is modest and not overwhelming, depending on what you see the host or hostess doing. In many cultural and ethnic groups, gesturing is a basic part of conversation, and you should feel comfortable doing so as long as everyone else is comfortable and you are being courteous to them. Of course, you should be conscious of the people sitting beside you—especially if the table settings are very close together—so that you do not inadvertently bump them with your gestures. One way to prevent making that error is to keep one hand in your lap and gesture only with the other hand. It tends to limit the range of motion and ensure that you do not hit anyone unintentionally.

However, when trying to get someone's attention, you should not point at a person or a thing on the table. Use your voice to draw attention to something or carefully describe the situation that you want people to observe or notice. In fact, during the dinner, you do not want to draw attention to yourself if you can avoid it. Focus on other people and what they are saying. The one exception might be when you need to excuse yourself.

Excusing Yourself

One of the major challenges in good table manners is what to do in awkward situations such as:

- Going to the bathroom
- Sneezing and coughing
- Hiccuping
- Getting something caught in your teeth
- Needing something from another room
- Leaving the table for a call
- Passing gas
- Needing to use a breath mint

The common solution to these situations involves excusing yourself—with the least fuss (no one needs to hear a general announcement)—and leaving with the least amount of attention and interruption of the meal. In some circles and in formal meals with children, people are expected to ask permission to leave the table. In that case, ask the host for permission to be excused. Otherwise, leave quietly and do not draw attention to yourself. When you leave the table, place your napkin on your seat, not on the table. Leaving it on the table—to the left of your plate—is an indication that you have completed the entire meal and are finished.

Do not place your napkin on your plate when leaving the table

When you have left the table, you can handle the situation in another room or the bathroom.

If you are caught with a cough or a sneeze at the dinner table, move your head away from the table, if at all possible, and cough or sneeze into your napkin so you don't sneeze or cough on anyone or the food. Then excuse yourself and wash your hands in the bathroom.

Burping at the table—a commonly accepted behavior in the Middle East, Asia, and among some ethnic groups—should be avoided in the United States unless you are entertaining visitors from a country where that practice is common. If you feel a burp coming and you cannot control it or stifle it, try to burp into your napkin while turning away from the table.

The rule of thumb—remember GRACE—is to be courteous to your fellow diners, appreciative of the host, and attentive about making your fellow guests comfortable. If you follow these practices, you will have made a contribution to a successful evening. As the dinner progresses, relax and enjoy it, and, when in doubt, follow the cues of the host.

Do not leave flatware loose on your plate at the end of the meal

Ending the Meal

One of the indications that you have finished eating—even if you leave food on your plate—is the way in which you leave your flatware. Normally, placing the fork and knife at four o'clock—with the fork tines facing toward ten o'clock and the knife blade facing into the plate—is an indication that you have finished the course; however, some recommend five o'clock and eleven o'clock. Resting the knife and fork on the plate at four o'clock ensures that they will not slide when being carried to the kitchen. (If you are British and used to eating continental style—where the fork stays in the left hand and the knife in the right—placing the knife and fork at nine o'clock and three o'clock is the indication that you are finished with eating that course.)

In formal dinner parties, where there are several courses, each one is cleared only when everyone is finished with that course, and then the next one is presented. There may be a palate-cleansing course—often a sorbet or something light such as a fruit or small piece of cheese—between two courses. At the end of the dessert course, it is typically time to leave the table. In private clubs and in some formal dinner parties, the group will often move to a different location for coffee and cordials or other beverages.

Leaving the Table

Normally, the host will provide a cue about when the dinner is over and it is time to leave the table. Sometimes, at informal parties, assistance in clearing the table and presenting dessert is appreciated, but most often you should remain in your seat. After the dessert is served—with or without coffee, tea, and dessert wines—and the conversation dies down, the host will invite people to another room for a beverage, or offer one at the table. If it is offered at the table, then you should expect to stay at the table.

Coffee and after-dinner drinks—dessert wines, cordials, liqueurs, and brandy—may be served at the table or in the living room. Alternatively, wine or highballs may be served, depending on the event and the entertaining style of the host. In these situations, accept graciously whatever you are offered and indicate your preference—if any—among options if offered a choice. If you are not interested in more alcoholic beverages, indicate that you would appreciate a glass of water.

Moving into the other room—often the living room or in private clubs the salon or another private room—offers you a chance to mix and mingle with other people beyond your immediate dinner companions. Thank them for their company as you leave the table and feel free to chat with other guests in this next phase of the evening.

Ending the Evening

At the end of a lovely evening—or earlier if you need to leave—it is appropriate to say good-bye and thank your host. You may also want to say good-bye to people you have met that evening for the first time, or share business cards and other contacts. However, it is not appropriate to make a scene or draw attention to yourself if you are leaving early. It makes other guests uncomfortable and may signal that they should leave. It also may make your host think you are not enjoying his hospitality.

Whenever you leave, thank your host but keep it short and simple. A sincere "thank you for a lovely evening" is often the most appreciated. Extra statements and overblown compliments are not necessary and constitute poor manners. If you really liked the evening, send a hand-written thank you note the next day to indicate your pleasure.

Thank You

Saying thank you is about recognizing and appreciating the care, work, energy, and expense involved in throwing a party, whether it is a dinner party, a celebratory party, or another special event.

The first and most important aspect of thanking is to remember to say it with conviction, honesty, and sensitivity at the moment of leaving the party. Express your appreciation for the food, the drinks, and the table presentation, and share other compliments. Mentioning a specific aspect of the evening provides a personal touch and demonstrates your enjoyment of the whole evening. A simple, honest, and truly felt "Thank you" will make a good impression. If you want to compliment the host but did not enjoy the meal or drinks, it is appropriate to say something such as, "Thank you for a special evening" or "I really enjoyed myself; thank you," or "I appreciate the invitation to dinner tonight. It means a lot to me to be invited."

Remember, however, to make only those statements that you can say honestly. That means that if you did not enjoy the meal, do not praise it or heap compliments on the host. Simply indicate that you really enjoyed the company. Speaking honestly will help you speak with conviction and prevent you from having to say something you do not mean; it can also help you avoid creating an awkward situation in which people remember your dishonest praise in the future. As Emily Post advised, "The really thoughtful guest thanks her host twice: once as she's leaving the party and again the next day. The written thank-you note is always, always appreciated, but is only expected after a formal dinner party or an overnight visit."

Of course, there are several ways to say thank you after the event—see the following sections on **Thank You Notes**, **Thank You Presents**, and **Thank You by Email**—but the most important statement is the one you make at the end of the evening.

Thank You Notes

One of the most powerful ways to make an impression involves sending a handwritten thank you note. Many people send thank you notes using email or instant messages; however, taking the time to handwrite and mail a simple note has a totally different impact. People recognize the time that you spent to find the right card, write a note, and mail it. Therefore, whenever possible, prepare a handwritten thank you note. It leaves a very positive impression and shows your appreciation for the event or party.

The note can be simple and direct. Write it in your handwriting, if it is legible. If not, print the message and sign it. Just say thank you once—not several times in the same note—and mention one particular element of the dinner that you enjoyed or that struck you as special. The note shows that you care about the person and appreciate the effort and care in preparing the meal and throwing the party. In fact, the thank you note can make a real difference. Recipients hold these notes, often read them slowly, treasure them, and tend to keep them, so they make a strong impression.

Although there is some debate about how long you have to send a thank you note— three days or a week—it is always important to send one. (Craig Claiborne gives you a week and Kate Spade three days.) When writing the note, make sure you have spelled all of the words correctly and that nothing is crossed out. If you are unsure about what you want to say, write a draft on scratch paper so that you can see how it will fit on a note card and review what you want to say or leave out.

If you are so inclined, add an interesting commemorative stamp to the envelope. You can purchase them at post offices. When you find one you like, buy several sheets so that you have them on hand to use when you need to write a thank you note.

Thank You Presents

In some situations, it is appropriate to send a small gift as a way of saying thank you. If you brought a hostess present when you went to dinner, sending a gift is not necessary. In fact, it may be way out of balance with the dinner party and often can make the host uncomfortable.

However, in situations where the party, or the visit, was extensive and you did not have an opportunity to bring a hostess present, then sending something personal along with a note is a very appropriate gesture. It is also very appropriate to send a present if you have stayed overnight or been a guest for longer than just the dinner party. If you broke something, soiled something, or otherwise made a big mess, you want to acknowledge that you created a problem. Providing a gift along with your note of apology shows that you recognize how far your host went to make you feel comfortable and that you appreciate his efforts and extensive hospitality.

You may have learned something about your host or his home that could translate into an appropriate gift. It may be something he mentioned such as a kitchen utensil, basket, vase, or dish. Or it may be something he never mentioned, but you noticed and think he might enjoy. Your gift may also be—but it does not always need to be—a replacement for an item you broke or damaged.

Another way to thank your host involves entertaining him. A gracious way to show him you enjoyed his hospitality is to invite him to a dinner party at your house. In that case, you are returning the favor of being entertained at his house. (For more information on hosting a dinner party, see **Chapter 3. Conduct Becoming a Host**.)

Thank You by Email

In situations where the host is a close friend, sending a quick thank you note by email is perfectly appropriate. In this increasingly technologically driven and socially mobile world, technology is not bad manners, but how you use it and what you say can be.

Some of the key rules about using email for thank you notes are avoiding ALL CAPITAL LETTERS, SINCE THEY ARE LIKE SPEAKING TOO LOUDLY OR SHOUTING, making sure that you fill out the subject line of the email so that the person knows what the email is about, using the person's name in the first line of the email, and signing the email.

Of course, if you said thank you during the event and thank you again as you left, it is not necessary to send a thank you note. It is often appreciated, but not required. It shows that you really enjoyed the evening and is an extra step that many guests do not take.

CHAPTER 3

Conduct Becoming a Host

This chapter examines what is involved in hosting a successful party. There are many elements to providing a good party, and there are manners involved in hosting a party. According to Craig Claiborne, although "good manners, like good taste, derive from sensibility and simple common sense, hosting involves more than simple common sense. It involves planning, arranging, and facilitating the entire evening."

Remember that your primary goal as a host is to make your guests comfortable so that everyone enjoys himself and has a good time.

Hosting

The most important part of any dinner party is the care and consideration of your guests. After all, you are having a dinner party for your guests to enjoy themselves and for you to enjoy the event yourself. Therefore, your ideas about the party should focus on what makes you and your guests comfortable. Wouldn't you like your guests to say, "There is no place I would rather be than here at this table enjoying delicious food, tasty wine, and the pleasures of engaging in interesting conversation"?

Therefore, think ahead about all aspects of the evening and decide what you want to do. It is your party, and you can make it any kind of party you want—something informal, something very fancy, and anything in between. Of course, if you are hosting a formal reception and using a reception line for people when they arrive, the plans and details will be dramatically different from inviting six to eight friends to dinner at your home.

The notion of hosting involves welcoming people to an event and watching over them to ensure that they are enjoying themselves. Greeting means taking their coats or showing them where to hang them, providing appropriate beverages and food, monitoring the conversation to avoid embarrassment or discomfort, and providing a delightful experience. In fact, when you consider all the aspects of hosting, it can be useful to make some notes and plans ahead of time. As Jeremiah Tower has written, "Your being a relaxed and hospitable host is the key to your guests' having a good time at your table. And it's all in the planning."

Planning should cover what you will serve—both cocktails and dinner—who will be invited, and where they will sit; how you will set and decorate the dining table; how you will organize the living room, terrace, or other setting; and what you will do to make the evening special. If you are used to hosting dinner parties, then planning can be fairly simple because it can become routine. However, it is always useful to review the list of items for which advance planning makes a real difference. For example, have you thought about:

- What theme, if any, do you want for the dinner party?
- How will you greet guests?
- Where will they place their coats and hats?
- Where will women place their purses?
- What alcoholic and nonalcoholic beverages will you serve for cocktails?
- What food items will you serve with cocktails?
- How will you serve them?
- How will people serve themselves?
- How will you decorate the living room or the space where you will serve cocktails?
- What will you serve for dinner?

- How many courses will you serve?
- What beverages will you serve with dinner?
- How will you decorate the table?
- How will you serve the meal (what style of service)?
- Who will sit where?
- How will you tell guests where to sit?
- How will you handle offers of help?
- What will you wear?
- How will what you wear contribute to the success of the dinner party?
- What other aspects of the dinner party need to be planned ahead?

Making notes about all these items helps ensure that you take care of them before the evening begins so that you can focus on your guests and make sure that they have a good time. Good planning also enables you to relax, enjoy the party, and follow the key principles of hosting.

Guidelines for Hosting

When considering the rules that govern hosting, there are five key guidelines to consider:
1. Courtesy
2. Comfort
3. Clarity
4. Convenience
5. Common Sense

Courtesy refers to the notion that you, as the host, should extend every courtesy to your guests, whether that means helping them with directions to get to your home or introducing them to everyone in the room and making initial connections. It includes providing appropriate beverages for the cocktail hour before dinner and ensuring that no one is left out of a conversation unless he chooses to be.

Being gracious or extending courtesy means inviting guests to a dinner with plenty of advance notice, whenever possible. (That does not mean you should not have a spontaneous dinner party. They can be great fun and easy for everyone; there is something mischievous and fun about calling people a day ahead or that day and asking them to come to dinner and to bring something you request. Some of the greatest dinner parties have occurred at the last moment.) It also means making sure that you have plenty of nonalcoholic beverages for guests who do not drink alcohol and the appropriate liquors, wines, and beers for those who do. It also means helping your guests understand your way of organizing a dinner party. If you are serving a three- or four-course dinner and have provided just a few hors d'oeuvres, describing the plan for the evening helps your guests relax and know what to expect. On the other hand, if you are going to host a two-to-three-hour cocktail party, it would be helpful to say, "We have a three-hour cocktail party before dinner, which is why you see so many hors d'oeuvres." These small acts of full disclosure can make a huge difference to the success of the evening.

Courtesy also refers to the notion that whenever you can help a new guest relax by explaining something—a task not necessary for your regular dinner guests—take the opportunity to do so. It will make that individual feel more relaxed. While this advice is especially relevant for people who have never attended one of your dinner parties, it is something to think about every time you host a party. Making people feel at ease is part of the role of a host, and being courteous is the best way to make sure that your guests enjoy the evening. It also encourages them to be courteous with one another.

Comfort means that your special role is to ensure that each and every guest is comfortable during the evening. That goal may mean providing detailed introductions, sharing background information when a story comes up that involved only part of the group, or ensuring that the food and beverages are appropriate to your guests. Serving pork or shrimp to some Jewish guests would be an affront, as would serving meat that is not halal to Muslims. It may mean steering the conversation away from a topic that might be too personal for some guests and introducing something more easily discussed. It involves thinking about what your guests want or might want, making arrangements to supply it, providing introductions for everyone, showing guests what to do with their coats, offering drinks, and giving instructions about seating. These items are all parts of ensuring guests' comfort.

Clarity means that the more the host provides information and the more the guests know what to expect or what to do, the better the evening will be. Explaining something about the evening ahead of time will prevent your guests from showing up for a backyard barbecue in a tie and coat, or arriving casually dressed to a formal dinner party with everyone in suits and ties or cocktail dresses, or being too early or too late. Coming in business casual clothes to a formal dinner party will make the guest feel very uncomfortable and many other guests uncomfortable, as well. Explaining the dress code to a person new to the area is good manners and helps that person fit into the event comfortably.

Consider possible allergies of your guests

Just as hosts or hostesses have the obligation to provide information to guests so that they know what the event will be like and how to behave, they also have the obligation to ask their guests ahead of time about serious dietary limitations or allergies—something easily done by asking, "Is there anything I should know about what you can or cannot eat?" (For more information, about these food issues, see **Chapter 8. Special Situations: Political Events, Dating Manners, and Very Formal Settings**.) This request will help prevent guests from the awkward situation of being faced with foods they cannot eat. Finding out that information, and then preparing the menu and selecting beverages accordingly, will make a big difference to your guests.

Provide table settings that indicate the style of the dinner party

A third area where clarity can make a difference involves the use of flatware at the table. In some situations, your guests may not know what style of dining you prefer. Indicating what fork or spoon to use for guests who look unsure or uncomfortable can help them relax and enjoy the dinner. Providing explicit—but not obvious or condescending—information about the number of courses, the use of utensils, and the use of side plates and wine glasses are other examples of how clarity can improve the pleasures of the evening.

Convenience—the consideration of what makes a dinner party easier for the participants—is another key aspect of hosting a successful dinner party. Convenience involves considering the guest list and ways to organize the dinner party so that it is easy for all the guests to participate in a relaxed manner. After all, your goal is to enable the guests to enjoy the conversations of the evening and the interactions with other guests. Therefore, spend some time in advance planning how to make the evening more convenient for your guests and especially for you, as the host. Making it easy for your guests to meet new people or reconnect with old friends, providing introductions for people you have not entertained before, and structuring the dinner seating to facilitate interactions are all elements of the art of hosting a successful dinner party.

The second part of convenience involves planning the menu and the evening so that it is easier on both you as a host and your guests. Providing a meal at a formal dinner table that includes raw oysters, artichokes, fondue, ribs, or lobsters in the shell can make eating awkward and inconvenient for many guests who are not typically prepared to eat with their hands at a dinner party. Making it hard for people to get a second glass of water or to reach the salt and pepper on the table also reduces the ease of the evening. Creating food items that require serving and clearing many dishes reduces your ability to focus on the guests, unless, of course, you have other people to cook, serve, and clean up the party. The inconvenience created when you have forgotten to provide bread and butter plates or enough spoons for the various items you are serving can also make enjoying the meal problematic. These situations happen when there is a lack of planning about how to make the meal convenient for your guests.

Common sense provides good guidance when hosting a dinner party. Common sense provides you with good advice about whom to invite (not the four people who do not like one another), what to serve (not something that will keep you in the kitchen the whole evening unless that location is where you like to entertain), and how to make the evening successful (not to overload it with too many agenda items). Think about who will come, how the evening will progress, and what you want to happen to create a wonderful and enjoyable evening.

Set the table for the evening you want to happen

Common sense also means thinking about what is likely to happen throughout the evening and deciding how to make it easier on every person. It means making sure that you have thought about serving dishes, chilled enough water (whether flat or sparkling), set out coffee cups and appropriate accompaniments, set the table with sufficient space for the style of service you plan, and laid out sufficient plates and utensils so that the evening will go smoothly. It is a matter of thinking through all the aspects of the predinner cocktails, the dinner itself, and the after-dinner activity. Sometimes common sense includes thinking about the menu and the ease—or difficulty—that guests may have with the food items. Other times, it means considering the ingredients used throughout the evening so that several items don't taste the same. Whenever you take the time to apply your common sense to all the elements of the dinner party and prepare appropriately, it will be an easier and more successful evening.

Although these five principles—courtesy, comfort, clarity, convenience, and common sense—provide general guidelines, there are specific details in successfully hosting a dinner party. The first and most critical decision you have to make—besides when—is whom you want to invite and why.

Invitations

When planning a party, one of the first things to think about is the purpose and people for the dinner party. What is the goal of your party? Are you trying to make new connections, introduce new people to one another, celebrate some event in your life or the life of one of your guests, start a new social group, or expand your business network? There are many possible reasons to hold a party. Some people do it to try out a new recipe or have fun with a new idea about food and beverage. Others host a party to repay social obligations. Others want to help some individuals get to know one another. Whatever your goal—and they are all valid and important—the chief factor to contemplate is whom you want to invite to the dinner and why. Some of the questions to consider when establishing a guest list include:

- Who do you want to spend the evening with?
- Who knows whom?
- Who is comfortable with whom?
- Whom might you want to introduce to new people?
- Whom would you want a new person to meet?
- Who will make the party successful?
- Whom do you need to invite to fulfill some social obligation?
- Who is single and who is partnered?

In all of these considerations, remember that you are planning a party to have a good evening, so think about the collection of individuals that will make the evening successful. If you must pay back others for having entertained you and you don't feel capable of making a successful dinner party, consider hosting a cocktail party instead. (For more information about cocktail parties, see **Chapter 5. Cocktail Party Manners**.) Remember that bringing new guests to your table often adds a special spark and more lively interest to the dinner party, since the other guests will want to get to know the unfamiliar guests. It also changes the dynamics of a group that has been enjoying one another's company for some time.

Once you have considered who is coming, then the question is how to invite them. The most common method is a form of invitation. For formal dinner parties, mailing a written, printed, or handwritten invitation is a way to provide all the information needed and indicate the tone of the dinner party. In less formal situations, sending an email, creating an evite, or making a phone call is just as effective and more common. In fact, evites are increasingly used since they are efficient, economical, and environmentally friendly, as well as an easy way to keep track of who has responded and who is planning to attend. They also enable your own creativity. Remember that an invitation serves many purposes:

- It sets the tone for the evening.
- It gives guests the time and location (and, if needed, directions to the location).
- It encourages guests to respond so that you know who is coming.
- It establishes dress code expectations for the event.
- It gives you a chance to indicate where guests can park or how they can most easily get to your home by public transportation.
- It indicates the level of the meal: is it a cocktail party with heavy hors d'oeuvres, a simple supper, an informal dinner, or a more formal dinner?
- It saves you from answering phone calls and emails about the event asking what to wear, when to arrive, and what to bring.

When the style or tone of the invitation matches the event, it makes it easier both for the guest and for you as host. For example, if you are hosting a very formal dinner party with black tie or dark suits and cocktail dresses, and you have people serving the dinner, the invitation will provide the words *Black Tie* or *Formal Dress* to alert guests as to how they should dress.

If you are hosting a special party, such as a birthday party, an anniversary, or a celebration event, you may want to send a special invitation. In that case, feel free to create your own invitation or use preprinted ones. Just remember to provide all pertinent data that your potential guests need to know, such as date, time, location, and any special information. Examples include ideas about gifts, dress code, or desired gifts (or no gift) for the guest of honor. (Wedding invitations are illustrations of the level of detail that you need to provide.)

If you are sending an invitation, you should request a response by a certain date. The most common way to request a response is to indicate RSVP followed by a phone number or email address. A less formal way is to write the phrase "Please respond by calling 222/333-4444 or emailing yourgoodhost@gmail.com.

An invitation also helps you gather knowledge that you need: who is coming, possible allergies (food, pets, beverages), dietary restrictions, and other issues.

Greet guests warmly when they arrive

Greeting Guests

One important way to set a tone for the evening and to make guests comfortable is to think about how to greet them. First and foremost, greet them warmly.

If they are arriving at your apartment or house for the first time, you may need to greet them personally so that they know where to go, what to do with their coats and their gifts, and so forth. For an informal dinner party, greeting them at the door or in response to the doorbell works out well. In a large, formal party with a doorman, that individual will greet them, take their coats, and usher them into the appropriate room. Then you are responsible for welcoming them into the living room or salon when they arrive (or are announced, in very formal occasions). However, if they are old friends, they can probably let themselves in.

Show your delight and appreciation for each hostess present

When you greet guests at the door, you may receive a gift. The proper way to receive it is to notice it, thank them, and take a cue from them about whether you should open it or just put it aside. (Often that option is up to you, but you may want to ask the guest about it.) In the case of a bottle of wine, thank them and put it aside. You do not need to drink it at the dinner party, but you can if they suggest it and if you can and want to accommodate their request. If you are serving a delicate meal and they brought a strong, full-bodied red wine, however, you may want to decline and indicate that you will save it for a special occasion. Remember that you have planned the dinner party and probably already picked the wines to match the food and may have already decanted the red wine (or wines) and do not need to incorporate their Gewürztraminer or Pinot Noir. Whatever the gift, thank them at the time and remember to thank them when they leave for the thoughtful (or appropriate or special or considerate) gift. (For more information on providing a hostess gift, see **Chapter 2. Conduct Becoming a Guest**.) Even if you do not like the gift you are given, or cannot imagine using it, thank them at the time and do it graciously. Remember that graciousness and consideration are always part of good hosting manners.

It is no secret that some hostess gifts are kept for regifting. They may be much more appropriate for a friend or family member, but you must regift carefully. Even though one person's trash can be another person's treasure, think carefully about how and when you regift a hostess present that you do not want. It is very embarrassing and hurtful to see something that you have given someone sitting on the table at another friend's house.

You do not need to send a thank you note for a hostess gift. Basically, the gift is a token indicating the guest's appreciation for the invitation and recognition of the work involved in making a successful party. Most of the time, thanking the guest at the time is sufficient. However, if a guest has brought an extraordinary gift or something that really made an impact on you, then you may send an email—a handwritten note would be even better—thanking them.

A key part of welcoming guests involves pronouncing names correctly and clearly. Remember the principle of clarity—pronounce names so that others can hear and shake hands (or kiss, hug, or bow, depending on your style or cultural expectations). Of course, you should introduce your guests to others in the room, either one-on-one if a large group, or as a group if there are not too many people in the room. In fact, one of the elements of introducing people is to help them get comfortable with one another. Therefore, providing some information is a helpful way of encouraging guests to start conversations.

Remember when introducing guests that it is far better to overintroduce than to underintroduce.

A second consideration in greeting guests involves offering drinks—a cocktail, an aperitif, a glass of sparkling wine, a glass of still wine, a glass of sparkling water, or a soda—that you have prepared or are offering for the evening. Being prepared to respond to those who cannot drink certain beverages, or who will ask for something different, is also part of planning for the evening. Remember the principle of comfort; you have probably considered what they might request. If you know what your guests like, then you are well prepared. If not, you can respond by asking, "How about a drink? Would you like a martini?" "Would you like a glass of champagne? Or would you prefer a glass of rosé?" or "Would you like a glass of scotch?" "Are you drinking red or white wine this evening?" "Can I offer you some sparkling water?" All questions indicate what you are offering. Giving your guests something to drink and inviting them to partake in the hors d'oeuvres (and, if necessary, explaining what they are) are all ways of greeting them and providing the message that you want them to be comfortable and enjoy the evening.

If you have set up a bar or beverage area, pointing that out to guests helps them get oriented. It also offers you the opportunity to indicate that you will get their first drink, but that they should feel free to help themselves to more. It relieves you of that task and enables them to see what the options are and to monitor their own choice of beverages and the quantity that they want to consume. Remember when setting up the bar area to provide nonalcoholic beverages (along with plenty of ice and lemons or limes for sparkling water) as well as alcoholic choices.

Play quiet background music during dinner

Another consideration in providing a warm environment for guests during the first part of a dinner party is the choice of music. Consider quiet background music that sets the tone. If it is too loud, guests cannot hear one another; if it is too soft, it is often provocative and inhibits conversation. The type of music also affects the group tone and ability to relate to one another.

Seating Guests

Developing a seating plan can be a formidable task; just ask anyone who has organized wedding seating, a large Thanksgiving dinner, or a large event with lots of different groups. You need to consider who you want to sit beside whom for a dinner party in your home to make the evening successful for each guest and figure out the impact of that seating arrangement. Even if you do not choose to use place cards, thinking about whom you want to sit where ahead of time makes it much easier when everyone arrives at the dinner table. Then you are prepared and do not have to stumble and make people wait—since they will ask where you would like them to sit. You will avoid an awkward period deciding who should sit where.

Some of the common strategies that successful hosts have used to organize seating include:

- Separating couples at the table so that they get to meet new people.
- Mixing the men and women so that they meet new people (at a dinner party with many same-sex couples, this issue is not possible and not relevant).
- Separating colleagues so that they get to meet new people and can avoid work conversation.
- Placing people with guests they don't know so that they get to know one another.
- Considering table size and structure when seating people who monopolize the conversation by putting them with people who also talk a lot or by putting them at the end of the table, where they can be more isolated.

Place the guest of honor to the right of the host, who sits at the end of the table—if the table has ends—and presides over the dinner; the seat to the right of the host is typically the place of honor. If you think you may need to control the conversation, you might want to sit in the middle of the table instead. If there is only one host, then the guest of honor can be seated to the right of that person or, alternatively, seated at the other end of the table. Some hosts offer guests the chance to sit where they want; that works with good friends who get together a lot and are comfortable with one another. It can also work with a smaller dinner party at which people can talk across the table when there is often one common conversation rather than many small ones.

In more formal dinner parties, you can provide place cards with names on them so that guests know where to sit, or simply indicate where they should sit as you escort them into the dining room.

Make sure that people are not crowded at your table; there is nothing worse than being so close to your neighbor that you cannot eat comfortably. You know the size of your dining table and how many people it can seat easily. That should be the number of people at your dinner party. If you need to measure, most dinner guests need about 26 inches of space not to feel crowded. If you are not sure, try putting two chairs together, sit in them with a friend, and measure the space that makes you two feel comfortable.

Put your napkin in your lap, not in your collar

Eating Dinner

As the host, you are the person to whom others look to see what to do and what to discuss. Some of the cues relate to use of napkins and utensils, some to topics of conversation, and some to level of formality. One of the cardinal rules of good manners is to follow the behavior of the host. In practice, that means guests wait for you to eat. In some cases, they will not put their napkins in their lap until you do so. To solve this problem, simply remove your napkin and place it in your lap as soon as you sit down. If you are serving, take the napkin and put it on your chair or beside your plate so that guests will know that they are expected to put their napkins in their laps. Guests also wait for your cues in case you want to say grace or otherwise introduce the dinner and set a tone. They will often wait to take a sip of the water or the wine until you do so. Therefore, it is important for you to be aware of providing these cues and doing so in a timely fashion.

Pour wine for your guests

Indicate when the meal should begin

In cases where you are serving plates from the head of the table, you may want to suggest that people begin to eat when they get a plate, but more often you will serve everyone first and then provide a cue for beginning to eat. If the dinner party is served family style, the guests will pass the dishes counterclockwise, serve themselves, and wait for your cue to begin. The critical action for you to take is to move your fork onto the plate, the universal cue that indicates that guests should now pick up that same fork and begin to eat their meals. You may not want to eat yet, but taking that action enables the guests to eat. It is important to do, especially if you are making sure everyone has what he or she needs. In informal or formal parties, you may need to return to the kitchen to fetch something that was forgotten or that a guest asked for and was not provided. You may go to the kitchen to find tools to clean up a mess or to return empty dishes. In both cases, it is helpful and good manners to move your fork onto your plate so that your guests can begin.

A second set of cues refers to initiating or clarifying the topic or topics of conversation for the evening, often by introducing them or indicating what you do not want discussed. Sometimes your guidance is explicit—as in, "Let's not talk about that topic tonight" or "I don't think we want to get into that topic with this group, don't you all agree?" It may also work to provide a dismissive look when a guest starts an unwelcome conversational topic. Many excellent hosts will have already thought about possible topics and start the dinner by introducing a topic by saying, "What do you think about xxxx?" and refer to a political or cultural event. It encourages individuals to talk and prompts the conversation, a critical part of any dinner party. As Craig Claiborne has said, "Good conversation is the essence of any dinner party. A host or hostess can plan a party perfectly down to the last detail, spending much time and considerable money, but without the energy and sizzle of the guests' conversation, the whole evening can turn into a lead-footed disaster."

Another aspect of leading the table is providing guidance about what to do—what level of formality you expect at your dinner table and how you want guests to behave. If you are comfortable with your guests using the British (or continental) style of eating—cutting and eating with the knife in the right hand and the fork in the left—then you may want to indicate that fact or simply not draw any attention to the way they eat. If you have provided side plates for bread and butter and for salad, you may want to point that out. If you plan a salad course after the main course, you may want to indicate that in conversation as well. Most dinner guests are excellent at reading cues. As the host, you are responsible for providing the cues around all aspects of the dinner and most especially the conversations you want.

Monitor and facilitate conversation

Starting and Facilitating Conversations

The purpose of the dinner party is to engage in interesting conversation, meet new people, enjoy old friends, enjoy one another, and have a great evening. Ironically, for all of the discussion about food preparation and presentation, the meal serves only to support the dinner table conversation. It is about dining and conversation, and not just epicurean delights. If the whole evening is just about "ooing" and "aahing" about the table and the food, the conversation will become inane, and the evening will turn boring very quickly. It is also bad manners to pay too much attention to the setting, the food, and the wine.

The key skills involved in starting the conversation are listening carefully to your guests, knowing their experiences or backgrounds, and being familiar with what they like to discuss. Some contemplation of these three elements before the party will help you serve as a better host and ensure that the evening runs well. Then you can introduce topics that you think will work with the assembled group and encourage them to engage. It will also help you avoid topics that will destroy the evening.

Guidelines for ensuring that all guests enjoy themselves include not reminiscing about experiences with some of the guests and isolating others unless you tell everyone the story. Another one is avoiding gossip—although there are some dinner parties that are all gossip by mutual agreement, and everyone knows all the characters. A third is avoiding topics that trigger strong emotions that lead to argumentative fights. Debates can be fun and invigorating so long as individuals honor and respect one another, but some topics with some individuals trigger very strong emotions, which can destroy the tone you are trying to establish and ruin the evening for yourself and many of your guests. A good rule of thumb is to pick topics that will trigger interesting conversation, even debate, among a wide range of your guests. Topics may include current events, analysis of political or sociological questions, local issues, and interesting people you have met. There are also many cultural events that lead to great conversations at dinner. Recent plays, movies, concerts, and books often lead to intriguing conversations and a range of opinions.

Challenges at Dinner

When hosting a dinner party, you may find yourself faced with various challenges that tax your knowledge of manners. They can involve a wide range of aberrant behaviors, including obnoxious guests, loud guests, guests who drink too much, guests who use their cell phones, guests who do not hear well, guests who spill beverages or food, guests falling asleep at the table, guests reaching across the table for something, and guests who break things. (For a more comprehensive list of problems at dinner parties, see **Chapter 7. Pet Peeves at Dinner Parties**.)

Hopefully, you will never have to face these situations, but in case you do, here are some friendly suggestions:

- Obnoxious guests can destroy the tone and ambience of a party. They can be overbearing, difficult to tone down, and often loud. Asking them to change their behavior might work, as most guests do not want to spoil a party. If the individual is sitting beside you, engage him in conversation, and focus the energy on you and not the table. If neither strategy works, solicit the assistance of fellow diners to help control the obnoxious guest.

- Loud guests can make the dinner party conversation difficult for participants. Most people do not like being yelled at, and you can request that the person use a softer voice, often reminding the person that you can hear what he is saying. If the behavior does not change, invite someone else to talk by saying, "We have heard your opinion, Pat, and now let's hear from Morgan."

- Guests who drink too much can also ruin the tone and feeling of the evening. Sometimes they get very quiet, sometimes they monopolize the conversation, and sometimes they just fall asleep. If a guest has had too much to drink, remember that you are liable for having served them too much liquor, and you should not let them drive home. The first step you need to take is to provide a lot of water or seltzer, and encourage the guest to drink that beverage, while also making sure that he does not consume any more alcohol.

Do not allow guests to use cell phones at the table

- Guests who use their cell phones at the table are becoming an increasingly wide-spread phenomenon. While that does not make it right, it is common. The first thing to do is to calmly and quietly—and personally and privately, if possible—ask a guest not to use his cell phone, iPad, or other electronic device at the table. (In business settings, this issue can be handled differently; see **Chapter 6. Manners in Business Settings**.) Another strategy involves suggesting that the guest leave the table and make the call or handle texts in another room. If that strategy does not work, you can say, "I don't think it is helpful to the evening for any of us to use cell phones during dinner. Don't you all agree?" In the case of a pending emergency or critical situation such as a sick parent or a sick child, you might reconsider and suggest that the guest keep the phone in his or her lap, put it on vibrate, and leave the table to receive a call.

- Guests who do not hear well can be difficult if they are continually talking to cover their hearing loss. However, turning off the background music and encouraging guests—quietly and personally—to speak up can often solve this problem. A little thought about where to place this guest, if you know about the hearing difficulty, can also mitigate this problem. Also be prepared to repeat your words often and clearly. Enunciate and move your mouth so that the guest can partially lip read—depending on the extent of the hearing loss. It can make a difference. Some hosts place a guest with a hearing challenge beside themselves so that they can speak clearly and loudly to the guest and forestall any hearing problems.

Simply ignore guests who fall asleep at the table

- Guests who fall asleep at the table, while very awkward, is not a common problem. The most gracious thing to do is ignore the individual unless he begins to snore. Then the individual's neighbor should be encouraged to wake him up unless she has already tried to do so. If the guest's neighbor is unsuccessful, then it is up to you to wake the individual and suggest he go lie down in another room or go home. Whichever solution you adopt should reflect your concern for all of the guests and not just the person who fell asleep. If it is early in the evening, then suggesting a nap in the other room—a guest room or other space—would return the focus to the discussion and the dinner. If the person has come with a friend or partner, you can invite the friend or partner to solve the problem and continue with the dinner.

- Guests reaching across the table for something can be strange to witness when you know it is not good manners. But the question is: Do you ignore it or say something? Since your goal as host is to make everyone comfortable, the most gracious response is to ignore it and keep the conversation moving, unless that person knocks something over. (For more information about this behavior and other similar gauche behaviors, see **Chapter 2. Conduct Becoming a Guest**.)

- Guests who dominate the conversation often destroy the enjoyment of the evening. It means that some people cannot make their own statements or contribute to the conversation. In this situation, invite the guest to ask his or her dinner partner something, or introduce a new topic and call on another guest to talk. If the dominating guest continues, graciously indicate that she has had a turn and invite other people to talk. In some situations, the guest may not be aware of his or her behavior, and a simple suggestion that others may want to participate may be sufficient. A second strategy is to develop a common question and indicate that you want to hear everyone's response to the question. It can be an issue of current events, a cultural point, politics, or comments about a concert, play, movie, or book.

Discourage guests from showing their pictures on phones

- Guests who show pictures on their phones during dinner have become more common. Some guests cannot imagine that there is anyone who does not want to see pictures of their animals, children, grandchildren, recent meal, or favorite trip. Reminding them that it is hard for everyone to see the pictures and inviting them to show the pictures at another time is one way to address this situation. Another is to indicate that cell phones and pictures make you—as the host—feel uncomfortable. These two strategies often work because guests do not want to demonstrate bad manners or be thought of as ill-mannered. If the behavior continues, invite the person to show the pictures in another room. Awareness of disrupting the party may be enough to eliminate this behavior. (For more information about other similar gauche behaviors, see **Chapter 2. Conduct Becoming a Guest**.)
- Guests who spill beverages or food can create frustration and a mess, especially when caused by reaching for something. Remembering to be gracious and courteous can help increase your patience while you work on cleaning up the mess and making light of the event. Being gracious also entails diminishing the importance of the accident and focusing on making the guest feel less guilty or embarrassed.

This list of challenges—while common—is not exhaustive and cannot cover all the situations that a host might encounter. However, the list does highlight the value of the five principles of courtesy, comfort, clarity, convenience, and common sense. Remembering and using them to guide your behavior will help you to be the perfect host.

Extending the Dinner Party

Typically, the dessert course, often served with coffee and tea—and sometimes with a dessert wine—serves as the end of the evening, but you may want it to continue. If you are comfortable with the company and want people to stay, invite your guests to leave the table and move to another room, such as the living room. (In traditional and formal settings, the women used to retire to a separate room—originally called the *withdrawing room*, which came to be called the *drawing room*—and the men remained in the dining room to drink cordials.) Remember to provide some information—consider the principle of clarity—about what you are doing. Make a range of beverage options available and indicate how long the conversation will be. Some hosts provide liqueurs, cordials, brandy, or after-dinner wines, as well as sparkling water. Others continue serving wine or coffee. You can do whatever you think is appropriate. It is, after all, your party.

Often your guests will be involved in a great conversation. If you do not want it to end, remain at the table. Simply clear the dessert dishes and flatware and bring glasses for the cordials or wine, which you will serve. If moving away from the table will interrupt the conversation, this strategy can be a successful way to continue the evening. More often than not, guests will choose to remain at the table. At some point in the evening, however, you may want your guests to leave.

Encouraging Guests to Leave

Sometimes you have given a great dinner party, and it is time for it to end, but no one makes a move to leave. Most guests—the well-mannered ones—will know to leave within forty-five minutes after dinner. In this case, you may want to let the conversation diminish and not add to it or encourage more participation. If you extend the evening and move the guests, you may find that the activity of moving from one room to another provides guests with the opportunity to check with their partner—often through eye contact—about going or staying and a way to leave graciously.

If guests indicate their intent to leave and offer thank-you comments, it is up to you to respond appropriately. If you want them to go, walk with them to the front door, where you can have a small visit or private conversation, and help them with their coats and hats. It is also a chance to make sure they know how to get home and are capable of getting there safely. It is also a time to thank them for their gift, thank them for coming, mention something they did to make the evening special—a comment they made, their contribution to an excellent conversation, the assistance they provided with the meal—so long as it is accurate and honest. As they leave, turn your attention quickly to others who are also leaving or who are staying.

If your guests do not seem to want to leave, and you are tired or want them to go, there are a number of strategies that you can employ and still demonstrate the fine art of good hosting. Ways to encourage guests to leave include providing information about the busy day you have tomorrow, mentioning the importance of good sleep, or refraining from refreshing glasses with more wine or water. You certainly have the right to indicate that the party is over. If you are still sitting at the dining table, start to clear the entire table as a cue that the evening is over. Others have ended dinner parties with gracious ending comments such as "It has been a wonderful evening, I enjoyed your company, and I thank you for responding to my invitation."

Other hosts and hostesses ask their guests what time they need to get up in the morning or what is on their schedule for the next day. Asking with real interest is a gracious way of continuing the conversation and subtly reminding them about what they may be planning to do tomorrow, which often triggers an awareness that they need to leave. Some guests just do not want to leave. In those cases, when everyone else or most of the guests have gone and you are not interested in entertaining anymore, you can tell the person that they need to go home, providing some reasons—you need your sleep, you have a lot to do the next day, you need to clean up. After all, you have worked hard to make the party successful. There is no reason to continue the party if you are not enjoying yourself.

CHAPTER 4

A Well-Set Table

The most important aspects of hosting a dinner party include serving good food and beverages to facilitate lively conversation. Setting a beautiful table makes guests comfortable and adds to the pleasure of the evening. The table does not need to be fancy and full of expensive items; it can be very simple. However, it is important to consider all the aspects of designing and decorating the table so that you can set it completely before the guests arrive; then all of the elements are prepared so that you and your guests can enjoy the evening.

Getting Started

For many of us, dinner parties are complex events that take a lot of planning and care, starting with who is coming and how you will seat them. Therefore, one of the first tasks in setting a table is determining the number of guests and the arrangement of guests at the table. Consider who will sit beside whom, why, what chairs will be used, and how the table will seat everyone comfortably. In business events, you may want to consider who you want to be near whom and why. At dinner parties, you may want to consider how large you want the group to be. At large family events or Thanksgiving dinners, you may have the challenge of where to seat people and how to create extra place settings. Often, that involves a children's table in another room or an extension of your dining room table. At your dinner parties, everyone should be seated at the same table, if at all possible.

Whatever the situation, place the chairs around the table first so that you can be sure that there is room for everyone; then you can decide upon a table covering and the details of each place setting. The challenge of arranging chairs around the table is to ensure that there is even spacing between them and that the table works for the number of people involved. As Arthur Inch, a proper English butler advised, "The most basic rule then and now is that there must be enough room for people to be at ease. . . . Actual space between chairs depends on the size of the chair." The size of the guests can make a big difference as well and needs to be considered when arranging chairs. While there is a range of very specific recommendations for the space between each place setting, they vary due to differences in table designs and chair widths. Recommendations for the distance between seats—measured from the center of each chair or place setting—include 18 to 24 inches, 24 inches, and 26 inches. The primary issue is making everyone comfortable; therefore, good hosts should sit in two chairs side by side before the dinner party to make sure that the seating pattern is comfortable and works.

Consider which chairs you will use and how you will arrange them. Think about the number of chairs you own and whether they match or complement each other. Often, you can make them work together by alternating different kinds of chair designs or different kinds of chairs. And you can use a different chair entirely for the head of the table or the guest of honor (if there is one).

There is nothing more awkward than a crowded table, or a table that has too much space between people. The crowded table—which sometimes cannot be avoided—can encourage a lot of conversation and sometimes makes dinner feel cozier. However, too much space between place settings diminishes the conversations, makes nuanced comments hard—since people need to speak so loudly—and drains the energy from the dining room. Therefore, consider the number of people and the size of the table, removing or adding leaves if possible to make the dinner table a better fit for all the guests.

Place seats at a sensible distance from one another

For informal parties, a runner down the middle of the table and place mats provide a beautiful look, or simply place mats alone. Even mismatched place mats can provide an interesting visual presentation at the table. Place mats work best when there is not a lot of flatware or crystal because most place mats do not provide enough space for a decent place setting. Since place mats show the top of the table, you will need a good-looking table surface; sometimes a bare table provides a lovely informal look for a dinner party. All of these options are good ones; it depends on the style and tone of the party and your resources as the host.

Consider using colors and unusual decorations to set a welcoming table

Designing a Beautiful Table

Considering that the first impression made on guests when they enter the dining room will be the design and placement of items on the dining table, think about what the table should look like. What image do you want to project with your dining room table decorations? Do you want the table to look formal and elegant? Seasonal and festive? Informal and casual? Do you want one primary color, a range of complementary colors, or contrasting colors? What impression do you want to make? How can the design of the table contribute to the comfort and delight of your guests? What cues about the dinner will the table setting make or obscure?

When considering the design of the table, many hosts begin with the china that they want to use and arrange the table linens, flatware, crystal, and decorations to complement the china. (The major difference between a family dinner and a dinner party is the quality of the china, glassware, linens, and flowers.) Most often, hosts decide on the tablecloth to set the style and tone of the design for the table. Regardless of which element of the table directs your design decisions, think about how you want the table to look and its impact on your guests. This issue remains the best place to start.

Once you have a sense of what you want the table to look like, consider what elements will be most important. Do you want to use candles? Flowers? Decorative items scattered around the table? A major centerpiece? Several centerpieces? An arrangement of scattered artifacts? Sometimes, scattering statues or articles collected from your travels provides an intriguing-looking table; the decorations provide something to admire and discuss during dinner. If they came from a particular country, do they match the food that will be served? They don't need to, though it is worth considering their function and how they will contribute to the enjoyment of the evening. However, as Craig Claiborne reminded hosts, "Resist the temptation to make your table setting the living embodiment of your ego, or a statement about your income. Your first consideration should be the comfort of your guests."

Since a range of collectible items—sea shells, colored stones, mosaics, small colored glasses, tiny vases, wooden or clay figurines—can be placed all over the table, they do not interfere with guests' ability to see one another—an important element of the table design. In fact, inexperienced hosts often fail to sit down at a table before completing the setup and do not realize until guests seat themselves that the beautiful flowers get in the way of good conversation, especially with small dinner parties. They often find themselves removing the decorations during dinner. Using a very tall candelabra or very low flower arrangements solves this problem.

Use flowers to make a pretty table

Use napkins and table runners for color

Napkins (and napkin rings) can also contribute a decorative touch to the table, making it distinctive and attractive. They often add a touch of color or a fascinating design, especially if the napkins are antique, unusual, or especially distinctive. When considering them, remember that they have to coordinate with the table linen, the china pattern, and often the crystal.

Centerpieces

Setting the table—beginning with a tablecloth or place mats and considering a centerpiece for the table—is a significant part of making the evening a success. A well-set table provides an invitation to conversation and enjoying the evening. It shows the dedication of the host to the dinner party and the guests, and it establishes the cues for the diners about what kind of evening it will be. As J. Rey, author of a 1920 book advising hostesses, wrote, "A novel scheme of decoration, so long as it is not bizarre, gives a dinner-party a good start. It provides the guests with something to talk about at once, which is 'half the battle.' It strikes a note of distinction and taste which puts every one into a harmonious frame of mind."

Very tall vases of flowers and large, elegant candelabra on the table signal a formal dinner. Conversation will most likely be limited to the people seated on either side of guests due to the centerpieces preventing conversation across the table.

Use candles as centerpieces to make a table shine

A lovely bouquet of flowers or set of artifacts on the table with each place setting means a more informal meal, one where the conversation can extend across the table.

Do not use centerpieces that are too tall

Do not use centerpieces that dominate the table

Use a lower centerpiece to facilitate conversation

Using candles as centerpieces can provide an intimate or formal look, and they do not block guests from looking across the table. When lit, they can also add a glow to the table and often add a festive look (as long as you are careful to select dripless candles).

The centerpiece of the table—or centerpieces, depending on the size of the table—should be appropriate to the formality of the meal and designed to focus attention on the evening. After all, it enhances the evening and should not dominate it. When deciding on a bowl of fruit or flowers or candelabra at the center, make sure to find the exact center of the table. In formal dinner parties, the flowers can be very tall—sometimes in vases that stand as much as 3 or 4 feet above the table—with matching candelabra; this structure works because formal dinners often take place around large tables and it may be impossible to talk across the table without raising your voice, so the decorations do not need to foster or allow cross-table talk. In more informal dinners, the centerpiece—whether flowers, bowls of fruit, or beautiful artifacts—should not be so high that it blocks the guests' faces from one another. Ten inches is an excellent height, and twelve inches should be a maximum, depending on the look of the table and the purpose of the evening. Other options include small bouquets of wildflowers, small bud vases of flowers, or small candles scattered throughout the table.

Present small gifts for everyone

After deciding on the centerpieces, consider table decorations at individual place settings or small gifts, depending on the nature of the party. In situations where the dinner party is celebrating someone's accomplishments or new situation in life, you may want to provide a gift to the guest or guests of honor. Or you may want to have a small gift for everyone. It is by no means necessary, but it builds anticipation and adds mystery to see small packages at each place setting. However, avoid adding too many items to the table, since they can detract from the beauty of a well-set table. As Emily Post wrote so beautifully, "Don't clutter place settings with decorative extras. Guests should not have to forage through table favors and other knickknacks to find their plates and utensils."

Consider using place plates, also known as chargers, to set the table

Placing Plates

Put plates on the table in the locations where you have placed the chairs. The plates put at each setting are called place plates, or chargers, to indicate where that person will sit, and they provide assistance in setting the table. Historically, decorative place plates were used in fancy homes to set the table and make a positive impression. Often place plates are fancy, beautiful, or special plates, which would be destroyed by a lot of use, and therefore, they mark the place setting but are not used for eating. They can also be simply elegant china in 12-inch size. Place plates are mostly used in formal settings and not in most informal dinner parties.

Typically, place plates are removed when the warmed dinner plates are put on the table, although sometimes they are used underneath the plates for the first course. Place plates are not used in most American households, even for special occasions, because they are seen as unnecessary and too fancy. If you are not using place, or charger, plates, simply set the table with the dinner plate and the other plates that will be used for the dinner.

The normal place setting for china is five pieces—the dinner plate, the salad plate, the bread and butter plate, and a cup and saucer—but not all of it is placed on the table at the same time. The salad plate is smaller than the dinner plate, and the bread and butter plate is smaller than the salad plate. In fancier settings, there is also a lunch plate, which is typically smaller than the regular ten-to-twelve-inch dinner plate. Soup bowls can be added to settings and can include a soup bowl, a rimmed bowl, or a cream soup bowl. Be sure to distinguish between coffee cups and tea cups, which tend to be smaller and wider (to help cool the tea) than coffee cups and come, like coffee cups, with their own saucer.

The dinner plate sits at the center of each place setting, while the bread and butter plate goes to the left of the dinner plate and, if there is room, on the same level. If not, it is placed to the left of the fork or above the fork so that it is still reachable on the left-hand side of the place setting. If both a bread and butter plate and a salad plate are used at the place setting, the bread and butter plate is kept closer to the rim of the table and below the salad plate. The bread and butter plate typically has a small bread knife on it, marking the top of the plate with the blade toward the center of the plate. This placement helps remind the guest that the knife is there for the bread and butter; there is no need to use a piece of flatware from the right-hand side of the dinner or place plate. If there is no bread and butter knife, the plate may be used for another purpose or the host intended the setting to be more informal.

Choosing the right bread and butter plate is easy because it comes as part of most dining sets. However, if you have plenty of china and want to make an aesthetic statement, combining various patterns by using a bread and butter plate that does not exactly match but complements the dinner plate can be an attractive way to set a table. Sometimes setting the table with a range of different types of china can bring a special tone to an informal dinner party. While inappropriate for a formal dinner, seeing several different sets of china or a range of different china plates often adds a touch of whimsy to the table setting.

If you have a hard time remembering where the bread and butter plate and the crystal go, touch your first finger to your thumb on each hand. You will see the letter "b" on the left hand and the letter "d" on the right hand. Bread and butter plates, "b," go on the left-hand side of the plate. Drinks, "d," go on the right-hand side.

The salad plate is typically placed on the dinner plate if the salad comes first in the meal. If it is to be eaten as part of the meal, the salad plate goes to the left of the dinner plate and on the same plane as the dinner plate. If the salad is served after the main course, the plates are placed in the center of the place setting, but only after the dinner plates have been removed.

Dessert plates are not typically put on the table, but they may be placed on a sideboard—if available—along with the coffee service. This arrangement makes it easier to clear the dinner service and provide the dessert service if the dessert service has already been chosen and is in the dining room.

Setting the Table with Flatware: Forks, Knives, and Spoons

Setting the table involves thinking about what utensils are necessary for each course of the dinner. If you are serving a soup, then the place setting needs soup spoons; if you are serving a salad as a separate course, then you need a salad fork and maybe even a salad knife. If you are serving an unusual item, such as fruit, which may require unusual pieces of flatware, then you need to take them from your collection, borrow them for the evening, or use a different but helpful other piece of flatware.

Place forks on the left and spoons on the right

Forks go on the left and knives and spoons on the right because most people are right-handed. Here's a helpful way to remember: there are four letters in L-E-F-T and four letters in F-O-R-K; the fork goes on the left-hand side of the plate. There are five letters in R-I-G-H-T and five letters in S-P-O-O-N and K-N-I-F-E; spoons and knives go on the right-hand side of the plate.

When setting several forks, knives, or spoons, remember that guests use them from the outside to the inside—within categories (forks, knives, and spoons)—or from the far left to the center and from the far right to the center. The process means that if the salad course comes first and calls for a fork and knife, the smaller fork—the one for the salad—is placed outside and to the left of the larger dinner fork. The same is true for the other side of the place setting. The salad knife is placed outside of the dinner knife, but inside the spoons because the tradition is to keep similar pieces of flatware together.

Setting the table with flatware involves knowing the menu for the evening and the utensils that will be required to eat the food easily and comfortably. Therefore, think about what you will need—at least a fork, knife, and spoon. For dessert you'll need another fork and spoon—placed horizontally above the plate with the spoon above the fork—and maybe several forks and knives and spoons depending on the number of courses. For a simple three-course meal with a first course, main course, and dessert, you will need to provide two forks (one for the appetizer course or the salad course—depending on the courses to be served—and one for dinner), two knives, one spoon, and the setting for dessert. (Remember that the flatware for coffee and tea is typically placed on the table along with the dessert plates and cups and saucers when dessert is served.)

Once you have determined the quantity of flatware needed, you need to decide on the type of flatware—will it be silver or stainless?—and then you can set the table appropriately. Start by adding the flatware to each setting and then return to each place setting to make the details even and symmetrical after the glasses have been placed. Normally, utensils are placed an inch from the plate so that the utensils can be clearly seen and admired as much as the plate. Finally, decide if you're setting the table American style—where the tines of the fork and the bowl of the spoon face up, the knife blade is aimed at the dinner plate, and the bread and butter knife blade faces the center of the bread and butter plate—or English style—where the tines of the fork and the bowl of the spoon face down to show off the silver marks.

Setting the table involves putting out what is needed but no more. The cleaner the look, the more easily the guests will know what to expect. Besides, you do not want to intimidate them since it is neither good manners nor good hospitality.

Place wine glasses to the right of the plate and above the knife and spoon

Placing Glasses

Glasses—typically called stemware due to the stem below the bowl on most wine glasses, champagne glasses, and water glasses—are placed on the right-hand side of the place setting and above the knives. (Remember "b" and "d.") The placement of stemware can be confusing, but it is not hard to figure out. Simply place the water goblet (or water glass) above and to the left of the knife and the wine glasses go to the right of the water glass or water goblet.

Place wine glasses in a row to the right and above the knife and spoon

If there are several wine glasses, they should be organized according to the order in which they will be used from the right (above the knife) to the center of the place setting. For example, if white wine is served with the first course, the white wine glass goes to the right of the water glass. The next wine glass—typically red but potentially another white wine glass—is placed between the white wine glass and the water goblet. Some hosts organize wine glasses in a curve from the top of the knife to the top of the center of the plate so that everyone can see what comes next. If you have good crystal, it also makes a nice presentation. If you don't want to make a curve or if there is insufficient room, arrange the glasses in a diamond shape with the water glass being one point, the last glass being the other point, and other glasses set between them.

The cardinal rule of good manners in organizing the wine glasses is to make them easy to reach and use. Since wine glasses are typically poured on the right side of the guest, placing the stemware on the right makes it easier for anyone pouring the wine. Therefore, the water goblet is placed farthest from the edge of the table and to the left of the wine glasses. Some hosts reverse this order and place the water goblet to the right of the wine glasses and closest to the edge of the table, because guests drink a lot of water these days. The order of wine glasses helps the guest know what glass to use and when and tells anyone serving wine what to pour into which glass.

In most parties—except formal ones—there is typically one wine served (or at most two). It is therefore easy to place the wine glasses on the table to the right of the water glass. The water glass can be crystal or a highball glass without a stem, depending on the look of the table and the kinds of glasses you have available for the meal. Often, highball glasses indicate that sparkling water will be served in addition to or in place of still water.

If you are serving several wines, set the table with all the appropriate wine glasses; their presence lets guests know what is coming, and it saves you from removing glasses and bringing new glasses to the table. If you are serving champagne for dessert, it will be the last glass in the row; otherwise, dessert glasses are left off the table and brought out—along with dessert plates and the coffee and tea service—when dessert is served.

Place napkins above the plates for decoration

Napkins

The choice of napkin should be done in connection with the tablecloth—the same color and material, a contrast, or a similar palate color. Then the decision is what special napkin fold to use with the napkins. There is no special rule for how to present napkins beyond making them accessible to guests, and there is no need to arrange them in fancy folds. (For information about how to make fancy napkin presentations such as stripes, the artichoke, the Bishop's miter, or the bird of paradise, see Lynn Rosen's *Elements of the Table: A Simple Guide for Hosts and Guests*.) In fact, one of the difficulties with a lot of folding is the amount of handling a napkin gets before a guest can put it in his lap. If you are going to make fancy folds, make sure your hands are freshly washed or wear gloves.

The napkin should be placed to the left of the dinner plate or on the dinner plate. It is sometimes placed under the fork and sometimes over the fork and on top of the plate. In fancier settings, the napkin can be placed on the place plate or in a glass in order to add color to the table and make a more aesthetic setting for dinner. In any case, the napkin quickly disappears when people sit down at the table; therefore, whatever location you chose will not continue to show during the dinner party. The napkin should be easily reachable. Placing it under a series of forks means that it is awkward to retrieve it; doing so makes a lot of noise and can disrupt the organization of the table.

A common way to isolate the napkin and add color or a design element to a dinner table is to use napkin rings. Besides adding decoration, they provide an easy way to present the napkin without going through a fancy folding process. Napkin rings also help guests easily access their napkin. If you use napkin rings, the napkin in the napkin ring can be placed on the plate or to the left of the plate. The only challenge can be where to put the napkin ring after the napkin is removed. Since they are normally placed on the table above the plate (and above the dessert fork and spoon), they add to decoration. They can, however, get in the way of the wine glasses if there are several.

Place Cards

In formal dinner parties or fancy situations, as the host, you may provide place cards—printed or handmade—indicating where your guests are supposed to sit. They help people find their seat and let you attend to other tasks at the busy time of final meal preparation and serving. Preparing them ahead of time also lets the host consider who to pair with whom so that the evening conversations go well and the guests enjoy themselves. Sometimes, seating decisions are critical because seating some people beside a particular individual can produce an unpleasant—even if memorable—evening.

Place cards can feel very formal and stuffy, but they can also be fun and add a touch of interest and intrigue to the evening. Creative place cards can carry forward a theme for the dinner—such as vegetable marking sticks for a farm-to-table dinner, colored eggs for Easter, little pumpkins and gourds for Thanksgiving or a fall harvest dinner, fresh grapes for a wine dinner, and chocolate candies for a Valentine's dinner—or they can be simple formal cards.

They should be placed above the center of the place plate or dinner plate. If there is no room there due to the abundance of glasses, they can be placed on the place plate or tucked into a napkin that is placed on the place plate. They do not last during dinner—and can be removed if needed—so their placement is not as critical as other items.

Serve from the guest's left side

Serving Styles and Serving Dishes

In modern dinner parties, there are four options for how to serve the meal: English service (host carving and serving), American style (plating food in the kitchen), family style (passing), and buffet (side-table serving). English service means that the meat or fish course, or the main items, and the side dishes are all placed in front of the host, who serves each guest in turn. In some cases, to speed up the process, the hostess seated at the other end of the table may serve the side dishes, or a guest sitting beside the host may be asked to serve the side dishes. This model works well when there is a clearly defined main dish or a few dishes. In many informal parties—and for many Thanksgiving and Thanksgiving-type meals with lots of dishes—several guests are given a dish to serve in the same manner as the host.

   In English service, the dishes will be arranged around the host at the head of the table. The host will ask each guest—in turn, starting with the guest of honor if there is one—for a plate and then serve the individual, often asking what the person wants and how much he wants of various foods. Sometimes, the host serves an adequate portion or with a clear sense of making the dish last to serve the number of people at the table. In this form of English service, guests pass their plates—one at a time when called on—to the host, who is serving. The host serves that person the vegetables or passes the plate to those providing the side dishes. In this manner, each person is served one at a time with everyone watching, and often commenting. This process provides guests with a great opportunity to make positive comments on the food, the colors, the aroma, or the choice. It is very appropriate to use this time for that purpose because it is often difficult to continue another conversational topic while plates are being passed around the table.

American-style service means that the plates are composed and served in the kitchen and brought to the table ready to eat. It takes a lot of organization for a host to arrange the plates and food items to serve all the plates equally and promptly while guests are waiting in the dining room. One option is to prepare all the plates in the kitchen and place them on the dining table before inviting people to sit. However, in most dinner parties, moving people to the table takes some time since it can interrupt conversations, and people sometimes take that moment to go to the restroom. The result is more confusion and often colder food. An advantage is the lovely display of beautifully composed plates that greet guests as they enter the dining room. It can be done after everyone comes to the table—which keeps the food hot—but it requires the absence of the host from the dining room while plating the food.

Plating in the kitchen also allows the host to ensure that everyone gets relatively equal portions of the food items and that the plates can be cleaned up a bit—with a wet napkin or paper towel—to be clean and presentable at the dinner table. Bringing the food out only after everyone has sat down ensures that the guests do not wait for the food and it does not get cold. After all, if you have spent some time preparing the meal, you want people to enjoy it. For dishes that are awkward to serve at the table—such as lasagna— serving in the kitchen can make the dinner party less messy and easier on everyone.

Family-style service for a dinner party means that the dishes are placed on the table in serving dishes. People pass them around and help themselves. Alternatively, if a dish is very hot or very heavy, a person near that dish might offer to serve others. However, if you want to use family service, it makes sense to provide serving dishes that are easy to pass; you might provide two dishes of the same food item to enable easy passing and ensure that everyone gets food at approximately the same time.

As a host, encourage people to pass the serving dishes to their right—in a counter-clockwise manner—in recognition of good manners and to avoid a traffic jam of serving dishes. As a guest, pick up a serving dish when requested and pass it to the next person on your right, never serving yourself first. Passing dishes in a counterclockwise manner—that is, to the person on your right—is the expected pattern and easier for most people because it is easier for most people to hold the dish in their left hand or put it on the table to the left of the plate and serve with the right hand. One variation is to offer the serving dish to the person on your left, then serve yourself, then pass it to the person on your right if the dishes are going counterclockwise (or in reverse if the dishes are going around clockwise). There will be plenty of time to serve yourself from the next dish that comes to you.

Increasingly, buffet service or side-table service means that the food items are arranged on a sideboard, and guests are encouraged to find their place setting—marked by a place card or the seat indicated by the host—and then pick up their plates and serve themselves from the sideboard. In this situation, the order of food begins with the main dish—meat or fish or the equivalent—and then proceeds with starches and vegetables. Condiments and sauces are typically placed on the dinner table for guests to serve themselves when they sit down and throughout the meal. Some hosts find buffet service much easier to organize, but it has the disadvantage of creating a line of people waiting to serve themselves, and many dining rooms do not have the room for a full table, sideboard, and plenty of space for a line beside and in front of the sideboard. Often, Thanksgiving and other holiday events are buffet service to save room at the table and to facilitate serving a lot of food. But remember that buffet service disrupts the flow of the evening and often slows down the process of guests obtaining food; it also leaves a messy sideboard for guests to notice. It often works better with family dinners or holidays as opposed to more formal dinner parties.

The most successful buffet service uses two lines so that guests can serve themselves from both sides of the table. It facilitates the speed with which people can serve themselves, and the food tends to stay hot longer. Unless you have hot plates or other mechanisms for keeping the serving dishes warm, two service lines can be an advantage. Of course, they take more space in the dining room. Buffet service can also be difficult for guests with allergies to some foods because it is often not clear, depending on what the host is serving, what ingredients are incorporated into each dish.

There are other service styles—butler service, Russian service, and French service—used when there are persons hired to prepare and serve the meal. Both butler and Russian service involve guests being presented with platters from the left side of the guest. In butler service, the staff person holds the platter and the guest serves himself from the platter to the plate. In Russian service, also known as platter service, the staff member serves the guest from the platter, which typically contains a meat or fish dish and accompanying vegetables. The guest indicates what and how much he or she wants, but the staff person does the work, also managing to make sure that there is plenty of the food to go around. French service, also called guéridon service, means that the food is prepared tableside; it is rarely done in private homes. Increasingly rare due to the cost, labor, and equipment needed, it can only be found in very high-class restaurants.

It is important to consider the issue of guest comfort in determining which style of service to use for a dinner party. English and family-style services are the most common because they can accommodate a dinner party more easily than the other forms, bring the focus of the guests to the table, and require less last-minute work in the kitchen for the host.

With each of these service options comes the expectation of a number of serving dishes. In both English and family-style service, hosts need a quantity of serving dishes and utensils for each of the parts of the menu and smaller dishes for condiments and sauces. There also need to be places to put these dishes during the dinner, one of the reasons not to set the table with lots of figurines, art pieces, decorations, and gifts. While there are many ways to solve a lack of space—including small side tables and removing empty dishes to the kitchen—considering what goes on the table and where it goes is part of the process of setting a table.

CHAPTER 5

Cocktail Party Manners

⋙

"The cocktail party is easily the worst invention since castor oil."
—Elsa Maxwell, American special events planner and hostess

"Cocktail party: A gathering held to enable forty people to talk about themselves at the same time. The man who remains after the liquor is gone is the host."
—Fred Allen, American comedian

Cocktail parties are a major form of entertaining in the United States, so understanding how to be a guest at a cocktail party and how to make the evening successful is a critical social skill. It is useful for both personal and professional purposes. (For more information about business settings, see **Chapter 9. Manners in Business Settings**.)

Types of Cocktail Parties

Cocktail parties range from the very casual and informal events that often happen in urban and suburban areas when you are spending time with people and you spontaneously invite them over for cocktails that evening to the formal cocktail party for which you have sent written invitations four to six weeks ahead. In between are the cocktail parties that happen before dinner parties when a large group of people are invited for cocktails and a smaller group are invited to stay for dinner. There are large cocktail parties to celebrate events and small cocktail parties to welcome people to the group. They are all valid ways of entertaining, and most of the rules are the same, with some minor exceptions.

There are lots of reasons to have a cocktail party. You might want to invite people to your home during a particular holiday season when the house is specially decorated (many hosts hold an annual holiday party), you might want to celebrate an anniversary or birthday (for yourself or one of your guests), or you may want to fulfill a lot of social obligations in one event. Perhaps you want to introduce someone new—a neighbor, your child's partner, a family member, a new colleague—to a range of people. Maybe you want to invite friends and colleagues to a cocktail party before a fund-raising event so that you ensure they attend the event and support your cause, or you may want to show off your new house, your new remodeling, or your new furniture. There are many reasons to host a cocktail party, and throwing a party can and should be fun. After all, it is called a cocktail party, not a cocktail mistake.

Thinking about what type of party you will throw, or to which you have been invited, is the crucial first step in planning. There are many ways to classify cocktail parties—by formality (which normally affects dress code), categories of guests, location, and purpose. The types of formality include:

- *Informal and casual (no tie and jacket for men; casual dress for women).* These events often include serve-yourself bars (sometimes with limited selections of liquor, wine, beer, and nonalcoholic beverages), food placed around the room, and few paid staff to help, if any. They are very comfortable and relaxed for most people because most guests will be familiar with the appropriate informal manners.

- *Business casual (open-collar shirt with sport coat for men; casual dress or pants and top for women).* These events often include self-serve bars (sometimes with limited selections of liquor, wine, beer, and nonalcoholic beverages) or bars with bartenders, depending on the size of the event; food placed around the room; and a few staff members who serve drinks and food.

- *Semiformal (tie and coat or suit for men and cocktail dress for women).* These more formal events often have full bars tended by professionals or people hired for the evening, finger food that is presented by staff circulating the party, and a musical group playing in the background.

- *Formal (black tie and tuxedo or dark suit for men and cocktail dress or formal floor-length dress for women).* These events include full-bar service, staff to provide drinks and cocktail party food, and staff circulating with food and drinks and cleaning up as they circulate. In these events, guests are expected to use proper and formal manners and often arrange with friends to dine together afterwards.

- *Very formal (white tie and tails for men with formal floor-length dresses for women).* These events include full-bar service, staff to provide drinks and cocktail party food, and staff circulating with food and drinks and cleaning up as they circulate. In these events, guests are expected to use proper and formal manners. In many of these situations—but not always—dinner is provided for a small group, or the whole group, after the cocktail party.

Another way to categorize cocktail parties revolves around the nature of the guests. Are they friends of yours whom you have known for some time or are they a group of colleagues for whom this event is a mandatory occasion? (For more information on business and professional events, see **Chapter 9. Manners in Business Settings**.)

Type can be also determined by location:

- At home without staff
- Catered in a home
- Garden party
- At a restaurant, hall, or club

If you are hosting a party, thinking about these categories will help you plan the cocktail party you want to have. If you are a guest, it helps to consider which type of party you are attending so that you can plan what you will wear, select an appropriate hostess gift, think about the manners you will need to be successful, and practice your behaviors, if needed. In any case, there is a lot to consider before showing up.

Before the Party

If you are planning a party, consider when and where to hold it and how to invite your guests, so that you give them plenty of information about the type of cocktail party you are holding. A written invitation—printed or handwritten—indicates a more formal party. An email invitation typically tells the guests that the party probably involves suit and tie, a cocktail dress, or the equivalent, or is more casual depending on the information in the email. A phone call invitation means that the event has not been planned way in advance and is more informal. However, it may be spontaneous but still formal, and you will be expected to wear cocktail party clothes. Of course, there are always exceptions to these guidelines because each host comes from a specific cultural or ethnic background and tradition, and can decide to do whatever he wants when throwing a cocktail party. If you know the host, you most likely know what the dress code will be; if you don't, feel free to ask someone else who is attending, or ask the host.

If you are invited to a cocktail party with a written invitation, you should respond promptly and honestly and then make sure you follow through on your decision to attend. It is rude and inconsiderate not to reply, because the host will not know how many guests to plan for. And it is equally rude and inconsiderate to say that you are attending and then not show up. The host may worry about you; he has committed to a certain number; and he probably looked to you as a favored guest at the party. When you see RSVP on the invitation, it means you should respond by the date given. If the invitation indicates regrets only, then you do not need to say that you are going, although a note to that effect is a considerate and appreciated gesture. For more formal parties, a written response is appropriate; for more informal parties, an email or a phone call suffices.

Eat carefully before attending a cocktail party

Before going to a cocktail party, consider what you have had to eat that day and make sure that you do not arrive with an empty stomach; it is the surest way to guarantee that alcohol will enter your bloodstream very quickly and may produce behaviors you might later regret. (One of the best buffers is a glass of milk and a peanut-butter-and-jelly sandwich because it offers a complete set of proteins.)

Entering the Party

Depending on the nature of the invitation to the party—cocktails at a specific time or cocktails from one time to another—you should plan to arrive on time or within an early part of the specified time frame, and not early. Most hosts prepare ahead for their cocktail parties, but there are often last-minute situations, and arriving early means that the host needs to pay attention to you instead of all of their other last-minute details. In fact, good manners means arriving within the first five to fifteen minutes of the time for which you were invited, but again, never early. The exception to this rule is if you are good friends of the host and can be helpful with last-minute arrangements and greeting guests. In that case, you should offer, ahead of time, to arrive fifteen minutes early.

Whenever you arrive, you should never make a major entrance. After all, you are neither the Duke nor Dutchess of Cambridge, Lady Gaga, Justin Bieber, Auntie Mame, or Woody Allen. You do not need to draw attention to yourself by making a grand entrance that stops the party. It destroys the rhythm of the party for the rest of the guests and indicates a self-centered approach to life that is a mark of poor manners. Unless the party is a costume party, simply arrive and greet the host.

You can greet the host in a variety of ways, depending on the style or the format of the party. In a very formal occasion such as a debutante or cotillion presentation, you may be expected to bow—or curtsey—as a form of greeting. However, the most common and acceptable form of greeting is to shake hands warmly and firmly, or hug the host if that is your style, while looking directly at your host and thanking him. Increasingly, hugs and kisses are becoming the standard form of greeting, but if you are not comfortable with that form of greeting, simply extend your hand. Typically, the host will indicate with his body language what type of greeting he prefers. Remember to take your cue from the behavior of the host.

Give the host your present—if you have one—and thank him for inviting you to the event. (For more information on hostess gifts, see **Chapter 2. Conduct Becoming a Guest.**) Put your coat in another room—unless there are staff members who take your coat—and check your outfit to make sure it still looks good. If at a formal or business event, make sure your business cards—called name cards in some cultures—are placed in your left-hand jacket pocket or left pants pocket or in an easy-to-reach location in your purse, so that you can easily retrieve them and give them to someone you meet. Locate the restroom so you don't have to interrupt the host to ask where it is when you need it. This early stage of the event is all about preparing to enjoy the party.

Do not use your phone during a cocktail party

This moment provides a good opportunity to turn your mobile phone off or at least turn it to vibrate. No one wants to hear your cell phone during a cocktail party, and it is rude to answer it when you are in conversation. The one exception is a pending emergency situation that you may need to respond to. In that case, tell the host that you are expecting an emergency call and might have to leave the room to answer the call or even leave the party. Notifying the host ahead of time makes it easier for you to leave in a hurry and prepares the host for the situation if it arises.

Greet your host or hostess warmly

Being Introduced

In formal cocktail parties, you may be introduced to a receiving line. In that case, you may be asked to present your card to a person responsible for announcing your presence to the receiving line. Alternatively, you may be asked to whisper—clearly and articulately—your name to the first person in the receiving line and that person will mention your name to the next person as they pass you along.

In large formal and diplomatic events, you may also be announced to the room after you have completed the receiving line. In other very formal situations where there is no receiving line, you may be asked to present your card so that you can be announced to the room as you enter. In either case, you will be asked to wait until the person in charge of announcing guests is prepared to announce you. He may ask for your card and will try to pronounce your name correctly. Don't correct him if he's wrong; simply proceed into the room and greet the people who come your way to say hello.

Greet and talk to a number of people

Mixing and Mingling

The point of a cocktail party is to mix and mingle and make new friends while renewing old acquaintances, so it is imperative that you work the room as a guest. In fact, part of good manners as a guest is to contribute to the success of the party by being a good conversationalist, talking to a number of people, and helping introduce individuals whenever the occasion arises. In addition, a work-related cocktail party offers you an opportunity to network. (For more information on networking, see the section on **Networking** in **Chapter 9. Manners in Business Settings**.)

Meet as many people as you can at a cocktail party

Shaking hands is an important part of meeting people in any setting, and it is especially true at cocktail parties. Therefore, go up to people and introduce yourself by extending your hand and saying, "Hello (or good evening), my name is xxxx." This action invites others to share their names and to shake your hand, thereby providing the beginning of a conversation. Jacqueline Whitmore, author of a book on business manners, says that "Today, handshaking is still a sign of goodwill and mutual respect. The type of handshake you extend speaks volumes about you and your intentions." In some circles, you are expected to hug the other person, and in ultra-chic New York City circles, blowing the "Park Avenue Kiss"—an air kiss to one side of a person's face and then to the other side, making sure not to touch the other person's face so you don't disturb makeup or touch the skin—is expected. Europeans often hug and kiss each other easily and comfortably; some Americans are not comfortable with these public forms of greeting.

When you shake a person's hand, do so firmly and with good eye contact. You do not need to make it a long handshake. Say something to the person such as, "A pleasure to meet you," or, "I have heard so much about you; I'm delighted, finally, to meet you in person." Choose words that work for you and that are authentic to the situation; do not manufacture them or fabricate a connection where there is none. Many people expect to encounter strangers at a cocktail party and are fine with a simple, honest greeting. Recognize the person as someone new and say, "My name is . . . and it is a pleasure to meet you." Then ask an interesting question. Do not treat a new acquaintance as if she were a long-lost friend. On the other hand, give the person some attention; don't ignore her just because she is new to you. (For more information about how to open and close conversations, see the section on **Making Conversation** in this chapter.)

In large cocktail parties, it may not be possible to shake hands with each person, especially when you are being introduced to a large group. In this situation, simply nod and give each person a genuine smile and then prepare to listen to the person who is talking. Good manners include listening; paying attention to others is a mark of good breeding and shows that you are honestly interested in other people. It is also a courtesy.

As you mix and mingle, join any conversation you want by simply walking up to a conversational group and listening. The rest of the group will probably invite you in by gesture and then introduce themselves if you are new. If they don't, feel free—when there is a pause in the conversation—to introduce yourself. If people aren't conversing when you join the group, you have the opportunity to introduce yourself to your neighbor on either side, which may start the conversation. Often, this activity will inspire the rest of the group to ask your name and introduce themselves. In fact, you may be helping others who find it difficult to introduce themselves or initiate a conversation. Introducing yourself is also a wonderful way to relearn people's names that you may have forgotten. By taking the initiative, you invite them to say their name, which helps you and everyone else remember them.

Join groups throughout the cocktail party

If you find it difficult to join a conversation, walk up to a small group and make eye contact with one person in that group. This is a signal that you want to join the discussion. Other nonverbal ways to join a group include standing in or near the circle or joining your spouse, partner, or date if he or she is already in the group.

A common way to start a conversation after the exchange of names is to ask how the person you're talking to knows the host. Alternatively, you can bring up a current event or a local issue. Remember that the purpose of mixing and mingling is to meet and get to know many people. Therefore, invite other people in your group to participate in a conversational topic by directly asking them their opinion. If they decline, graciously accept their desire not to participate.

As you participate in the conversational groups during the cocktail party, remember to listen well, ask genuine questions, and contribute to the conversation. However, do not dominate the conversation without an invitation. When you are new to a group, the group members may ask you a number of questions. In that situation, you may be the focus of conversation, and dominating it is appropriate. However, you can always find a way to turn the conversation around to the other people by asking them to answer the question that you have just answered. This action shows that you have a genuine interest in other people and that you want to get to know them. It also takes the focus away from you.

Getting away from a group of people that no longer interest you or moving on so that you can meet other guests can be challenging. You can implement any of the following four disengagement strategies or invent your own:

- Excuse yourself, indicating that you need to go to the bathroom or to the bar to get another drink. Even if you don't, it is a gracious way to leave. However, do not offer to refresh anyone's drink unless you want to return to the group. Otherwise, you will have to come back and you will have failed to find a gracious way to leave.

- Say that your date, spouse, or partner—or the host or hostess—is beckoning to you. Make sure you go to that person even if the individual was not trying to get your attention.

- Tell the group that you want to meet a range of people. Say that you made a promise to yourself to do that, you are expected to do that, or that it is part of the fun of a cocktail party for you. Simply say, "Thank you, I have enjoyed the conversation, but I promised myself I would meet as many people as I could tonight. I look forward to seeing you again later."

- Say, "It has been a pleasure talking with you," and then simply move away.

These gracious ways to leave a group do not hurt anyone's feelings and demonstrate your consideration for others.

The rudest way to transition to a new conversation is to just leave a group and make a beeline across the room to someone you would rather be with. One way to avoid being rude is to make sure to say good-bye—in a simple and gracious manner—to the people you are chatting with. Remember that most people expect to mix and mingle at a cocktail party, so you should not feel guilty about leaving one group for another.

Exchange business cards at cocktail parties if asked

If the cocktail party is a business or professional function (such as a business mixer or business card exchange) and you want to be able to contact the person you are meeting later, you can ask for a business card and present your card in return. To facilitate the process, keep your cards in an easy-to-reach pocket or location in your purse so that the cards can be exchanged easily. When you receive the card, look at it carefully, thank the person, and put the card in a pocket. In Asian cultures, admire the card and hold it; putting it away too soon is considered offensive. You may also want to use the person's name when thanking them. It helps you remember the name and gives you a chance to pronounce it. In addition, using the person's name, which you may have forgotten in the discussion, helps you when saying good-bye. With the business card, you are saved from asking the person's full name again.

If the other person does not have a card, offer your business card and ask them to write their contact information on the back. Make sure you read it so that you know what it says. There is nothing more frustrating than finding later that you cannot decipher what was written on the back of your card. When you have reviewed the card, put it in a pocket separate from the one holding your cards. You don't want to lose this card, since it has the guest's contact information.

Eating

One of the most awkward parts of a cocktail party involves eating the canapés or hors d'oeuvres that have been prepared for your pleasure. The key principle of managing food and drink at a cocktail party involves holding the food and drink in your left hand to leave the right one free to shake hands. This task is much simpler if you have a stemmed glass, because it is easy to hold. It also prevents the heat from your hand from warming the wine too much. Perhaps more importantly, holding the wine below the bowl gives you more control; if you get jostled or bumped, you will be able to prevent spilling wine on your clothing or on the people next to you. The best-case scenario is being provided with a plate notched to hold a wine glass and recessed to hold hors d'oeuvres food. Regardless of the shape of your beverage glass, however, remember to keep it in your left hand throughout the evening.

Hold food and drink in left hand

If canapés or hors d'oeuvres are being passed, take one with your free hand—typically your right hand, since the left hand holds the beverage—and eat it promptly. Most often this finger food is easy to consume in one bite. Remember also to take a napkin, and if you want to keep it, put it in your left hand with the drink. Then you can always find it if you need it, and it still keeps your right hand free to shake hands or help yourself to more food.

Although most hosts try very hard to create easy-to-eat finger food, you may be offered food that you don't know how to eat. In this case, you have several choices: ask the server what the food is and how to eat it, watch what others do, or pass on the item. You can also take the item and try a small bite, putting the rest in the napkin in your hand if you do not want to finish it. Then simply fold the napkin to hide the food and dispose of the napkin promptly.

Do not double-dip into sauces

If you use a spoon or toothpick, do not use it a second time for food safety reasons. Simply place the used spoon or toothpick in the receptacle for that purpose near the food, fold it into a napkin that you keep in your hand, or find a way to dispose of it unobtrusively. If hors d'oeuvres are being passed, staff members will be glad to collect your dirty napkins and used spoons and toothpicks. If there is sauce provided for a canapé or hors d'oeuvre, you get only one chance to dip the food into the sauce. Do not dip shrimp, wings, or other food into the sauce, take a bite, and then dip the rest of the food again.

Not only does it contaminate the sauce, but it is also an example of extremely poor manners and a disregard for other guests.

If, during the process of eating, your hands or fingers get covered with food, simply wipe them well with a clean napkin. If you have a lot of food on your hands or they have an aroma, excuse yourself to go to the restroom and wash your hands.

Sometimes, canapés or hors d'oeuvres require two hands. In that case, before you take the lamb chop or the spring roll, put your glass on a nearby table top or counter space. Eat the food, enjoy it, and then retrieve your glass. If you look for your glass and cannot tell which one might be yours or if you lose your glass for one reason or another, simply excuse yourself and obtain a fresh, clean glass with the beverage you were drinking. It is far better to use more glasses than to drink out of someone else's glass, unless you are discussing a particular drink and the person drinking offers you a taste. In this situation, take a sip if you want, return the glass, and then continue the discussion of the bouquet and taste of the beverage. If you do not want to taste the drink, simply say, "no thank you," and decline.

Not Drinking Alcohol

If you do not drink alcohol, ask for or find a nonalcoholic beverage and sip it during the party. You should not feel any pressure to drink alcohol when you do not want to. Not having a drink in your hand can make a host uncomfortable. Holding sparkling water, a soft drink, or another beverage—whatever your pleasure—makes you part of the party. If you are not comfortable being around others who drink, do not accept an invitation to a cocktail party. There is no need to put yourself in an uncomfortable situation where you will not enjoy yourself.

However, if you attend the cocktail party, remember that it is not appropriate to lecture others about their drinking and the problems it may create. A cocktail party is a place to have fun and enjoy the company of others—not a place to preach about any particular topic. Of course, if someone asks why you do not drink, feel free to share whatever part of your story or your reasons that you are comfortable discussing, so long as the story is brief. If the issue is private and you do not want to explain anything, simply say you have a headache or you are taking some medicines that do not interact well with alcohol—cold and flu medicines often fit this description. No one needs to know more. Or ask what they are drinking and if that drink is a favorite of theirs. Switching topics by asking about them or what they are doing is a very useful and considerate strategy when you do not want to talk about a particular topic.

Enjoy yourself at cocktail parties

Making Conversation

The purpose of a cocktail party is to meet new people, make new friends, and enjoy the company of old friends, so you will want to engage in good conversation. While making and sustaining good conversation is a real art, you can start with the following guidelines.

The first principle is to prepare before attending the party. Take some time to read newspapers, news magazines, or information on the Web so that you have something to discuss. Think about what movies or plays you have recently seen or what concerts you have attended. Think about vacations you have taken and what you liked or disliked about them. On your way to the party, review possible topics that you want to talk about or that you are prepared to discuss. This time also gives you a chance to review whom you want to meet—if you know the guest list—and what you would like to learn about them.

The second principle is to find a way to overcome your natural shyness—more people are shy than most people realize—by practicing some introductory lines. Use these lines when you greet your host and the people you know well, which can help to remove any nervousness. The simple act of going up to strangers and introducing yourself can also help you—and other people—feel more comfortable. Starting the introduction process helps everyone.

If you have a difficult time starting a conversation, remember that most guests are looking for a good conversational topic. If you have a good topic to start the conversation, they will appreciate your efforts. Some of the most common topics to use include: the weather; vacations, either recent ones or planned future ones; the décor; current events, whether local, regional, national, or international; recent movies, plays, lectures, or concerts; charitable causes; favorite or unusual restaurants; and current and timely books. Once a conversation has been started, you can ask more questions that invite others to talk, remembering always to ask the questions in an honest, curious, noncritical manner. Useful questions include:

- Why did you go there?
- What was special about that trip?
- What friends or people would you recommend to go there?
- Where are you going next?
- Why to that location?
- What do you think the government should do about xxxx (pick any current topic)?
- Why do you think that?
- Why does that topic interest you?
- How did the movie (or concert or play) compare with what you expected?
- What was the lecture about?
- What museum exhibits have you recently seen?
- What concerts have you recently attended?
- What are some of your favorite causes?
- What have you been doing to advance that organization?
- Weren't you at the recent gala? Charitable event?
- When did you move your office?
- What have you been thinking about since that lecture?
- What is your favorite local restaurant?
- What restaurant do you frequent most often?
- What books are you reading these days?
- What do you like about the book? Dislike about the book?
- Will you read his or her other books?

While this list may be useful, avoid introducing topics such as parenting, pets, religion, and politics. The parenting and pet conversations eliminate some people from the conversation who then feel awkward if they do not have children or pets, and they trigger others to tell you—in intricate detail, complete with pictures from their cell phones—about their child's or grandchild's most recent accomplishment. Religious and political conversations can evoke strong feelings that may be problematic at a cocktail party, even though the topics may be wonderful for a group seated at dinner. Sometimes, they generate thoughtful and respectful discussion; other times, they trigger strong emotions and aggressive debate. When in doubt, trust your intuition.

Drink less than you want and enjoy it more

Drinking

A cocktail party is a place to have fun, relax, meet new people, expand your network, and enjoy yourself. It is not a place to drink too much alcohol, no matter what the situation. A good rule of thumb is to drink less than you want and less than you regularly do. You can sip or water down your drink. No one wants a drunk or tipsy guest who slurs his words at the party. Drinking plenty of water—flat or sparkling—is also a good way to enjoy the cocktail party. Many people who attend lots of cocktail parties start with a glass of sparkling water to hydrate their system. This strategy works well if you expect to be at the cocktail party for a long time, especially if it appears that there will not be a lot of food to eat.

Another strategy is to fill your glass only halfway. You will cut down on the amount you drink and also help prevent spills on yourself or others.

To prepare yourself for a cocktail party, make sure you sleep and eat well before arriving at the event. People who have not eaten much food that day or who are tired are more easily affected by alcohol. If you have not eaten or slept well, consider refraining from alcohol at the beginning of the party; alternate every alcoholic drink with a glass of water, sparking water, or a soft drink; or dilute your liquor with a mixer and plenty of ice.

Remember that most bodies absorb alcohol at a relatively slow rate. People with less body weight absorb alcohol faster. In fact, the liver absorbs only one standard drink— 1.25 ounces of liquor, 12 ounces of beer, and 4 to 5 ounces of wine—per hour. Keep in mind that fruit punches hide the flavor of alcohol and enter the bloodstream very quickly, as do hot drinks. Alcoholic drinks mixed with fruit juice can easily lead to overconsumption.

If you feel intoxicated at a cocktail party, stop drinking liquor, wine, and beer and switch to soft drinks or water. If that does not help, your body is telling you that it is time to leave the party. Remember, however, that you do not want to drive with too much alcohol in your system. It is better to call a taxicab or ride-sharing service or find a ride with a friend than to drive with alcohol in your system. You can also appoint a designated driver ahead of time.

Leaving the Cocktail Party

You should leave a cocktail party before it has come to a complete end. Try to leave a half hour before the scheduled end of the party. If you are involved in a great conversation, complete it and thank your fellow guests before finding the host to thank him. Or try to leave when you see a large number of guests heading for the door. Leaving when you—or your spouse, partner, or date—has had enough to drink is always a good guideline as well. Normally, proper manners indicate that guests should leave while they are still having a great time and the party is a success.

Of course, if you are good friends with the host and you normally stay after the guests leave to help clean up and visit, then you should remain at the party, but you can start to pick up glasses and detritus while the last people are leaving.

Part of leaving is finding the host and thanking him for the cocktail party. Be sure to offer an honest compliment as well as a thank you. If you intend to see the host again, indicate that fact. You can also say that you hope to have him come to your house sometime, but only offer this comment if you really mean it. You may find that it's hard to properly say good-bye to both the host and hostess if there were two. In that situation, saying good-bye and thank you to only one of them is appropriate, and you can always follow up with a note of thanks later. It is poor manners to stand around waiting for one of them to break away from a good conversation or from finishing a task in order to talk with you. In that case, leave unobtrusively and remember to send a legible handwritten thank you note. (For more information about handwritten notes, see the section on **Thank You Notes** in **Chapter 2. Conduct Becoming a Guest**.)

CHAPTER 6

Manners in Business Settings

"Prepare yourself for the world, as the athletes used to do for their exercise; oil your mind and your manners, to give them the necessary suppleness and flexibility; strength alone will not do."

—Lord Chesterfield, British statesman and author

Manners in business settings are similar to the manners described in the previous chapters. Because business events occur at receptions, special events, meals, and cocktail parties, they build on the manners previously discussed. This chapter shows you how to adapt the manners you already know to business events and meetings.

The Setting

Manners in business settings vary with the situation and the context, but there are some common elements. A business setting is a place where you want to accomplish certain goals, whether they include obtaining business, expanding business, acquiring new contacts, or celebrating success. In these situations, you want everyone to feel comfortable, and you want to demonstrate your basic respect for other people so that you can focus on the matter at hand and accomplish your goals. Therefore, the focus of manners should be to enhance and enable the conversations, to diminish difficulties and obstacles, and to make a connection with each person you meet. To make these meetings successful, think about how you dress, how you talk, what you eat and drink, and how you make the event successful for everyone, regardless of whether you are hosting the meeting or just participating. Because long-term personal and professional relationships are central to successful business enterprises, consider what you can do to make the event beneficial for everyone involved.

The second common element of business events to remember is that people come together to make or deepen relationships and to expand their contacts, so you need to present yourself well in these events. Because it is all about networking, you need to show that you have knowledge of and a command of good manners, superb interpersonal skills, and attentiveness to others. Dress, language, and behavior are the critical aspects of your presentation of self. As Jacqueline Whitmore wrote, "The first rule of networking is visibility. In order for people to know who you are, you must see and be seen." And you want to be seen in a positive way. Depending on the nature of the business meeting or event, your preparation may differ.

Manners are essential to the successful conduct of business. As Amy Vanderbilt wrote, "It is highly desirable from a social and business point of view for every man to know and practice the accepted manners of his time—to err, perhaps on the side of punctiliousness in such things." Good manners make a difference in obtaining employment, advancing your career, building relationships, and increasing business opportunities.

Types of Business Events

There are several types of business events and meetings. Each has its own business function and agenda. Each also has its own protocol and appropriate manners, although most manners are similar across a wide variety of business events. Knowing the differences among them will help you prepare appropriately and use manners relevant to the setting.

Prepare to do business at casual luncheons

A casual business lunch: These occasions are often places where real business is conducted, often between or among managers and executives and in a setting that enables work to be done. Sometimes these events are intimate lunches or dinners—sometimes even power breakfasts—with just a few people working on a specific deal or customer. Other times they can be large dinner events with a number of people in a private dining room. In these settings, proper dress, language use, and formal table manners are critical to the success of the event.

Program or new product launches: While very specialized, these events are important to an organization, and everyone plays an essential role in making them successful. They require awareness of rituals, protocol, and congratulatory behavior as well as proper professional manners.

Trade business cards to build a future relationship

Business receptions: These events include cocktail parties, business card exchanges, and other networking opportunities. Remember that you do not want to embarrass yourself, your department, your colleagues, or your company in any way. That means holding back on what you might normally drink so that you are sober, focused, attentive to others, and adept at networking.

Project or planning meetings: These events often happen in small group meetings on a regular basis, sometimes involving food and beverage, especially during periods of launching a project, reaching certain milestones, and completing the work. Professional dress and behavior as well as good table manners are both essential and expected.

Prospect review events: At these events, potential hires or potential business partners are "interviewed" and introduced to others within the company. The agenda typically involves sensing or measuring the fit between the individuals, companies, or organizations and the culture of each company. It is not unusual for a candidate for a major position to be invited to several breakfast events, luncheon meetings, or dinner parties in order to assess the match. At these events, your knowledge of and skill in using manners and your level of comfort with various situations are being assessed.

Conferences, conventions, and trade shows: A significant amount of business is conducted at conferences, trade shows, and conventions. In these situations, you represent your company, are often required to wear a certain uniform, and are expected to act in a certain way. Attending a conference to grow professionally may seem to have a more personal focus; however, while you participate in these events, you represent your organization and are expected to demonstrate good manners and professional behavior at all times.

Celebration events: Many businesses hold events to honor corporate accomplishments, the success of a team in completing an important project, special individual endeavors, or anniversaries. These types of events can range from huge corporate meetings and very large sales events to small dinners or receptions with just the individuals involved. Corporate culture and tradition set the pattern for what happens and often mandate that certain activities happen in a prescribed order. Attending these events is a wonderful way to experience the corporate culture, make or renew contacts in the organization, and applaud your colleagues. These events demand knowing good manners and using high-quality interpersonal skills.

Introduction meetings: These situations involve getting to know new people as colleagues, building teamwork, and assessing individuals for a variety of circumstances. Your attentiveness, oral memory, good manners, and sense of etiquette will make a real difference in these meetings.

Fund-raising or charity events: As part of a company, you may be invited—or expected—to attend charity events as part of a group. Often the company will purchase a table; let you know the date, time, and location; and expect you to represent the company at that event. It is critical, therefore, to know how to participate in these events and to understand what is expected.

In all of these settings, you will be expected to meet new people and introduce yourself, a significant and often underappreciated networking skill. You are also a representative of the company or organization that is your employer; recognizing their traditions and *modus operandi* is part of being a member of a team and is considered proper behavior and good manners. Because what is expected as good manners in one company may differ in another one, it is your job to learn the rituals and expectations of your employer and to follow them graciously and hospitably. It is also your obligation to network with the people you meet in any business setting.

Shake hands with everyone at networking events

Networking

Networking is one of the most important functions of business events. The first principle of networking involves giving, not taking. Many people consider networking a way to make connections with others so that they can do something for you, but that notion is backwards. Networking is about making connections so that you can do something for others. Focus on giving and not getting! Giving can be as simple as providing introductions to others, sharing something that you have read or found, or assisting the other person in numerous ways. As you prepare to network, consider these six guidelines:

1. *Make friends first:* focus on engaging the person, not on what will happen. Treat networking as a journey to enjoy with a friend, not a goal to accomplish.

2. *Think of networking as farming, not hunting:* that means cultivating relationships, not harvesting them.

3. *Focus on the other person:* networking is about making positive connections and increasing the engagement of those connections.

4. *Help others first and you will eventually help yourself:* if you help others and focus on them, you will find that you will be rewarded many times over.

5. *Plan ahead like a sailor for networking situations:* chart your courses before networking by thinking about whom you will meet, what you want to say, and what you can do for these people.

6. *Remember that everyone you meet is a potential relationship:* you never know who will help you and how; the world is a small place, and, amazingly, people do not forget.

Don't be a wallflower at a business reception

The first part of networking means reaching out to other people—making eye contact, showing interest in the other person, and smiling in a genuine manner—being a wallflower or a reluctant participant will not help you. In order to network, you need to introduce yourself clearly and obtain contact information from the other person. That means explaining what you do, what projects you are involved in, what interests you as a professional, and what outside interests you are pursuing or want to pursue. In a way, you need to be able to give the person you want to meet or engage with information about yourself—a short, appropriate, and well-prepared elevator speech—so that you can pursue the connection after the business event. In most situations, the other person will be glad to listen to your elevator speech, and it may spark some good questions and an interesting conversation as well as further connections.

The second part involves obtaining information about the other person, most importantly the person's name, pronounced properly, and contact information. It is amazing how many people do not bother to learn how to say another person's name with respect! Hopefully, you can exchange business cards, because this method is a quick and very efficient way to share contact information. Another method is to send contact information from one smart phone to another, a very appropriate way to use technology in these settings (though not at the dinner table).

The third part of networking is remembering people and maintaining connections over time. As Jacqueline Whitmore reminds her readers, "Because we live in a fast-paced, often impersonal era, it's more critical than ever to offer the little niceties that might easily be forgotten, yet make other people feel important or appreciated. Little things such as smiling and cheerfully greeting a coworker, remembering a client's name or his children's names, or asking about someone's ailing friend or family members, establishes a rapport that eventually leads to stronger business relationships." Therefore, the more information you can learn about a colleague, the easier it is to show that you care about them. Be sure to use this information carefully and sensitively as you follow up to build and maintain a working relationship.

Introductions

The first place to start thinking about manners in business settings involves making and responding to introductions: how you introduce yourself to new people, how you respond to other people being introduced to you, and how you ensure that everyone else knows one another. To accomplish these goals, prepare for the meeting by reviewing the names and titles—or positions—of all the people you know are attending the meeting. Reviewing the names and backgrounds of these people will help you make conversation and introduce people to one another. You may want to research the people at the meeting by Googling them, checking on them on LinkedIn, or asking—discreetly—people who might know them pertinent questions. In fact, the better your preparation, the more successful and pleasant the meeting will be for you and everyone involved.

The second part of preparation involves placing plenty of business cards where you can easily reach them while shaking hands with a new person. Put them in your left jacket pocket, left dress pocket, or easily accessible purse location (or left pants pocket if no coat or blazer) so that you can reach with one hand and shake with the other. One way to make this process easier is to avoid drinking any beverage, thereby leaving your left hand free to hand out a card while you are shaking hands with the right. That way you can introduce yourself, shake someone's hand, and provide the person with a business card, which reinforces your name, all at the same time. It helps make the introductions easier and shows that you care enough to help others learn your name and your position in a gracious manner.

When you arrive at the event, take some responsibility for making people comfortable. Even if it is not your meeting or event, you can help make it a success by greeting people with a warm and firm handshake, welcoming them, helping them find their way, and explaining the protocol of the meeting. Playing a welcoming role will give everyone a positive impression of your abilities to meet and greet and support the meeting. You get to be seen as a winner, and the other person gets to be more comfortable and happier with the situation. As Letitia Baldridge, Chief of Staff for Jackie Kennedy when she was First Lady, wrote, "The art of meeting and greeting people with charm and efficiency is one of the most effective tools with which anyone in business or the professions can be armed." Sadly, this skill has been disappearing in everyday business and professional settings; that makes it even more important and distinctive for you to be good at and comfortable with it.

If you are attending a very formal business dinner or diplomatic event, learn the protocol for introducing people in this setting. These days, this formal structure is often ignored in favor of a more democratic model, where everyone introduces everyone else in order to help each person feel comfortable. However, when in doubt, introduce people lower in position or rank to those higher in position, younger people to older people, members of your company to guests or clients, and peers to peers. If you are not sure what to do, follow the cues of the host or meeting organizer. Always remember that the goal of introductions is to make sure that everyone is introduced and no one is left out. It is better to overintroduce people than to underintroduce them.

Do not hug people inappropriately

Meeting and Greeting

At the beginning of most business meetings, the host or organizer introduces people who do not know one another. At this time, you should shake the person's hand, hug them (but not inappropriately), or bow to them, depending on their cultural background and the culture of your company. If you do not know what to do, observe the behavior of people around you. If you prefer to shake hands, offer your hand and provide a firm, friendly, and short handshake while smiling and making eye contact with your new acquaintance. As Emily Post described this process: "Remember, a handshake is an offer of friendship. If your grip is really weak (the 'dead fish') you'll appear cold and disinterested. A bone crusher, however, can cause injury—hardly a friendly gesture—and it does not prove anything. Don't exaggerate hand shaking—it should move through a range of about five to six inches. Finally, don't place your free hand on top of the clasped hands or clasp the other person's wrist, as both of the gestures express dominance." Despite what Emily Post has said, the two-hand handshake has become a gesture of warm connection, not just dominance, in many business settings. It is up to you to decide how you want to shake hands with your colleagues.

Do not greet a person with a crusher handshake

Greeting new people is also a good time to use your name and to ask for and use the other person's name; using it will help you remember it, and you won't have to ask for it again later. If you do not hear the name clearly, ask again and pronounce it until you get it right. Take the time to get the name right. It is far more difficult later not to be able to use the name accurately. If you can't remember a person's name, feel free to ask for it again. You can avoid embarrassment in the future by learning the name now. In addition, knowing a person's name shows respect, and doing so may distinguish you from your colleagues.

When meeting someone, introduce yourself first and then present your business card. When you receive the other person's card, read it carefully and pronounce the name correctly a few times—another way to help you learn and remember the individual's name. (For more information on meeting and greeting, see the section **Entering the Party** in **Chapter 5. Cocktail Party Manners**.)

Introducing yourself carefully, warmly, respectfully, and professionally is the hallmark of a well-mannered business person. Successful business people use the occasion of meeting someone new to learn something from that person. They are very good at asking questions, drawing the individual out, and encouraging them to speak about themselves. They are aware that they never know who might be useful and important in the future.

Wear your badge on your right side

Badges

You may be provided with a name tag at professional and business conferences and cocktail parties, hopefully prepared ahead of time so that it is legible. (In most situations where badges or name tags are used, the first name is printed large and the last name small so that it is easy for a person to read it.) If so, accept your name tag and wear it on your right side so that a person shaking your hand can read it without having to look across your body. It is not appropriate to place a name tag on your waist or in another location where colleagues can't read it. It can lead to an awkward situation where someone is trying to read your name tag but looks like they are examining your body.

Do not wear name badges too low

There are a number of ways to affix the name tag to your outfit. The clip can be attached to a collar or the edge of a coat, blazer, sweater, or shirt. If there is a pin, you can use it to pin the badge to your clothing on the right side of your body and high enough that it is readable. Sometimes, name badges come with lanyards or chains. In this situation, put it over your head and adjust the length so that it sits comfortably on your chest. Remember that the goal is to enable people to read your name easily and without strain. If you do not see a pin or a chain, ask for one—but avoid long chains that position name tags in a way that draws more attention to body parts than to names.

Even if you do not like them, use name tags if they're available. They make it easy to mix and mingle and may save you from the embarrassing situation of remembering a face, but not a name. They enable other people to use your name comfortably. They also leave you free to focus on other aspects of good manners at business events.

Principles of Manners at Business Events

Just as there are common elements of manners as a guest or a host, there are foundational aspects of manners in business settings. They include the concepts of **C**omfort, **A**ppreciation, **R**elevance, and **E**tiquette, which can best be remembered by the acronym CARE.

Comfort is about the ease and manner with which you conduct yourself and your ways of making others feel comfortable in the setting. In business events, your ability to exude confidence is a mark of your professionalism and good breeding (unless you want to dominate others because you are the person in charge and want to use your power over others). The first principle involves caring about the comfort of your guests if you are the host and the comfort of your host if you are a guest. No one wants to feel uneasy at a business event.

Appreciation is the concept of thanking the host, the meeting organizer, the people at the business event, and the staff for the event. Having good manners means noticing what was done to make the meeting or event successful and showing appreciation for the work involved. It also means appreciating, in a genuine and sincere manner, the accomplishments of individuals and groups. Their success is something to celebrate. Doing so in a positive and authentic manner is the mark of a successful business person and part of one's good manners in any business setting.

Relevance refers to the type of occasion and the demands of that situation. Very formal events are different from casual ones, and the manners often change in detail, if not in principle. Behavior that is relevant in one setting is dysfunctional and inappropriate in another. A challenging business negotiation calls for a very different set of manners and behaviors from a more relaxed situation where you and your colleagues are celebrating an accomplishment. Compare the applause—and sometimes even singing—at a corporate sales meeting in a huge ballroom with the quiet tone of an elegant dinner in a private dining room for an executive who is being honored by his colleagues. Remember that the expression of manners—but not the principles of good manners—varies with the situation and the people involved.

Etiquette refers to recognizing traditional ways of doing things, honoring the hierarchy of the organization, and respecting the positions of the persons involved. It includes realizing there is a protocol to business meetings—whatever size or kind—and successfully operating within that protocol. It benefits you to learn the code of behavior and to honor it; to do otherwise makes your presence more public than you want it to be and in ways that may not be helpful to you in the long run. Therefore, learn the company procedures and rituals by observing carefully the behavior of those around you and incorporating the patterns of behavior into your repertoire. In some companies, gentlemen are expected to open doors and pull chairs for women; other companies consider the behavior sexist. Some companies expect managers to be addressed by title and last name; others insist on first names. Whatever your company does should become your practice.

Following these principles reminds you that when invited to—or told you will—attend a business meeting that involves food and beverage, you should respond in a positive manner and promptly. It is rude to withhold your response as if waiting for a better offer. If you have a conflict in your schedule and you cannot attend, you should inform the person who invited you, thereby making room available for another person. If you accept, and another business demand intrudes on the scheduled event, you will have to decide which takes precedence. In social situations, the earliest booked event takes priority over newer invitations, but in business the demands of customers or clients may require your presence and cause you to miss a company event. If you must cancel, you owe the event organizer the earliest notice that you can provide.

Along with the expectation to respond promptly to an invitation, you should also send a prompt thank you note after the meeting to your host or the meeting organizer, especially if the meeting was a dinner or other more personal, significant event. A simple email thank-you to the organizer for including you at a launch meeting, charity event, awards dinner, or reception can suffice, but for a small dinner party or an interview, a legible, handwritten note—mailed promptly—is good manners. (For more information about thank you notes, see the sections on **Thank You** and **Thank You Notes** in **Chapter 2. Conduct Becoming a Guest**.)

Besides responding promptly to the invitation to a business meeting, event, cocktail party, or dinner, you should arrange your schedule and travel situation so that you arrive on time—if not a bit early. In the world of business, arriving on time is arriving late. No one wants to wait for a single individual even if he or she is the guest of honor. If the meal serves as an interview, you should be a few minutes early. However, too early—more than fifteen minutes—shows no consideration for the host or organizer and the last-minute arrangements that need to be made. Arriving late shows an equal disregard for the valuable time of the host and the rest of the group.

Be careful not to choose your seat—wait for your host

Seating at a Business Event

Seating can be a simple matter or a very confusing one at a business event. It all depends on the protocol and the situation. In large events, when you are part of a table purchased by the business and you represent the company, you will sit at the table assigned to you. The highest-ranking official from the company will determine where you sit at the table. He or she will indicate where you should sit or give you permission to sit at any place at the table. If there are no instructions and the table is round, which is often true of banquets, then you can take whatever seat you prefer. Once you have guidance, you can take your seat, read the menu and other materials placed at the table, and greet those already seated.

Shaking hands and introducing yourself to everyone at the table is a gracious thing to do and often essential because you may not know the guests at your table. It is also a way to start conversations and set the tone for the rest of the evening. Making introductions by using your name first and then your position and company also helps others who may recognize you by sight but may not be able to remember your name due to a lack of regular contact, a difference in outfits, or the lack of a context. It is another way to show that you know and can demonstrate the principles of CARE—**C**omfort, **A**ppreciation, **R**elevance, and **E**tiquette. (For more information on CARE, see the section **Principles of Manners at Business Events**.)

Introduce yourself to your tablemates

If you are someone's guest at a large fund-raising event or other function, take your cues from your host. Depending on the type of event and the structure of the cocktail party or reception beforehand, you may not see your host until you all arrive at the table. If you arrive at the table first, make sure that you do not claim a seat until the host indicates where people should sit. If the host is delayed, make sure that the seats with the best sight lines to the front of the ballroom where the program is being held are reserved for the host. The rest of you can arrange yourself accordingly with the guests of honor—if there are any—closest to the host.

Move your chairs to see and hear the dinner speaker

When the program begins, you can move your chair in order to see the stage or front of the hall. If you need to move your chair, apologize to neighbors or others at the table before moving so that they understand what you are doing and why. (You don't want them to think you're moving to get away from them.) This statement is also a gracious way to acknowledge that you will be sitting with your back to them, not a normal seating arrangement.

Selecting Menu Items at Business Events

In a business setting, you need to consider several principles when ordering food and drink. First, order items with some regard for the prices on the menu. Most hosts do not expect that you will order several courses and select the most expensive entrée available, and thinking that is what you should do is foolish. Select from the middle range of prices something you'll enjoy eating and ask if others are ordering first courses. Sometimes the host has chosen the menu. If he hasn't, consider his suggestions, since he may be familiar with dishes for which that restaurant is well known. Remember, however, that you do not have to order something that you have never eaten, that you dislike, or that is hard to eat.

Second, think about the process of eating the food that you order. You might really enjoy chef's salads or pasta dishes, but they are notoriously difficult to eat in settings where people are paying attention to your table manners. They can also be messy. You don't want pasta sauce on your shirt, you don't want to fumble with artichokes, and you don't want to make a mess of food that requires you to use your hands. Therefore, order only items that are easy to eat, since you want to impress the people around you. If you have a choice of items, select ones that need little knife work and that you don't eat with your hands. Order only foods that you have eaten before or know how to eat. Nothing makes a business meal more awkward than an individual who doesn't know what to do with his or her napkin, flatware, crystal, or food that's difficult to eat. A good rule for business meals is to order food that is easy to eat with a knife and fork, even if there are items on the menu that you would prefer.

Avoid the following foods, which can be difficult to eat:
- Artichokes and other vegetables that require using your hands
- Chicken wings
- French onion soup
- Fruits that have not been prepared for eating with a fork and knife
- Mussels, clams, or lobster that require you to use your hands
- Onion rings (order if you are prepared to eat them with a fork)
- Oversized sandwiches
- Pasta with sauces that are difficult to eat
- Pizza (order if you are prepared to eat with a fork and knife)
- Ribs and other meats that contain bones
- Whole fish
- French fried potatoes (order if you are prepared to eat them with a fork)

Third, observe the host and follow cues about the meal. You should be able to figure out how long in time he wants the meal to be, how long you should expect to be present, how much you will eat, how many courses will be served, what kinds of beverages are appropriate, and within which price range you should be ordering.

In terms of beverages, a good rule of thumb for a first meeting with a business colleague—for an interview, promotion, or reassignment—is to forego any type of alcoholic beverage, especially at lunch. If your host orders a drink, you can demur and order water, sparkling water, iced tea, iced coffee, a soft drink, or another beverage. And it is acceptable to stick with your decision even if you are encouraged to order a drink. In an interview situation, you need to keep your wits about you and be ready for any question or situation you may encounter.

If you are relaxing with colleagues and not working in an official venue, then you can consider an alcoholic beverage—or more than one—but it is always a good idea not to drink during the middle of the day. Keep the alcohol for later, after work when you are spending time with your peers—and not your supervisor. In these relaxed situations, you can order what you want as long as you are comfortable in your relationship with professional colleagues.

If the meal involves a buffet, you still need to mind your manners. It is entirely appropriate to review the items on the buffet to see what you might like and what you will put on your plate. Because most buffet lines start with salads and end with entrées, you should determine what the main course will be and plan what you want to eat so you don't overload your plate. If you cannot see the food due to the line of people at the buffet, observe what other people are serving themselves. Their choices may give you ideas about what you want. After you serve yourself, return the serving utensils to their appropriate place—a dish or plate designed to hold the spoon, fork, or tongs—and use only the utensils for the food for which they are designated.

Never bring a used plate back to the buffet. Either leave your plate on the table for service staff to remove or place it on a side tray and pick up a new plate for your second time through the buffet line. It is neither sanitary nor good manners, in a restaurant or other commercial establishment, to bring a plate from which food has been eaten to the buffet.

Serve yourself less than you want. You can always return to the buffet line, but piling your plate high with lots of food makes it awkward to eat and makes you appear gluttonous, an impression you do not want to create.

Do not pile your buffet plate with too much food

Your behavior at a buffet is as important as any other aspect of your behavior at a business meal. Just remember: if you want the job or the contract, eat simply, comfortably, and graciously.

Dress Codes

Put thought into your choice of clothing and accessories for a business meal. Most business events are conducted during the day or just after work—although they are really a continuation of the workday—so people often expect to attend in business dress. That means that your normal business dress would be appropriate. In other words, come in a suit and tie for men or dressy blouse and pants or suit for women with appropriately dressy shoes and accessories, although nothing too showy. The rule of thumb for dressing for these events is to blend into the group but not to look too bland or too outrageously dressed—which is a real challenge.

One way for women to meet that challenge is to change accessories or scarves between the workday and the event; for men, it might involve changing a tie or putting one on. As in networking, you want to be noticed—for all the right reasons—so that people will remember you. Remember, though, that the best presentation of self starts with a clean, well-pressed, and professional outfit.

Table Manners

The rules for good table manners are the same as for dinner parties (see **Chapter 2. Conduct Becoming a Guest**) with some variations. That means that you should enjoy the meal if you are a guest, follow the cues provided by the host, refrain from drawing attention to yourself, and engage individuals—or the group, if appropriate—in interesting conversation. Watching your manners is also important because no one wants to eat with a slob or a show-off. Therefore, monitor your manners and do not make a spectacle of yourself. Reading and remembering the following twenty rules will help you display the principles of good manners.

1. Take your cues for what to do from the person in charge of the event.
2. Keep your napkin in your lap.
3. Serve others before yourself.
4. Do not talk with your mouth full.

Do not talk with your mouth full

5. Do not make inappropriate noises at the table.

6. Do not pick your teeth at the table.
7. Do not eat too quickly.
8. Do not cough at the table.
9. Do not interrupt other people when they are talking.
10. Pass the salt and pepper together.
11. Do not season your food before tasting it.
12. Eat your food only when invited or when everyone is served.

Do not cough at the table

13. Ask for what you need in a polite and respectful tone.
14. Do not ask for more food; wait for it to be offered.
15. Do not monopolize the conversation (even if you are being interviewed).
16. Do not point out or mock other people's manners.
17. Do not point with flatware (especially with food on the fork, knife, or spoon).
18. Do not blow your nose into your napkin.
19. Do not eat with your hands (even if invited to do so).
20. Wait for everyone to finish before expecting the dish to be cleared.

Some of these guidelines are meant for every situation, but some apply differently in various settings. For example, you should avoid eating with your fingers at restaurants and business dinners.

Do not eat with improper flatware

Do not eat with your fingers

It is very poor manners to pick up your lamb chop, pork chop, chicken bones, or steak bones with your hands and try to get every last morsel of meat. Use your flatware to cut off what you can and leave the rest on the plate. However, if you are in a casual setting, such as a company barbecue, it is perfectly appropriate to eat pizza, southern fried chicken, french fries, hamburgers, and potato chips using your hands. In that setting, you would look odd using a fork and knife. But in a formal dinner setting, you are expected to eat the potatoes, pasta, or rice with your fork and knife (or chopsticks if appropriate and provided), even if the meal includes french fried potatoes. Even hamburgers served in a formal setting should be eaten with a fork and knife, which may mean separating the meat and fixings from the bun.

Hosting a Business Meal

When hosting a business meeting that involves a meal, make arrangements for the meal with the restaurant or hotel and decide on the menu or provide guests with the opportunity to select from a limited number of menu items. The beverages—still water, sparking water, and wine—should also be picked ahead of time, if at all possible. Cocktails, if appropriate, can be ordered at the time of the meal. If there is a policy on nonalcoholic beverages at meetings, the host or event organizer should provide that information to the restaurant to avoid awkward situations; as the host, you can simply offer your guests water, soft drinks, juice, or other nonalcoholic beverages and expect your guests to pick up on the cue.

If you are the host, you also need to determine whether the event is Dutch treat (everyone pays his or her own tab)—an unusual but increasingly acceptable practice—or if the company is picking up the bill. You need to decide how the bill will be paid; how to handle gifts, coats, and other issues; and who will sit with whom. You may also want to set expectations for use of mobile phones. If the meal is Dutch treat, you must indicate that fact to your guests ahead of time, especially in business situations where the expectation is that the boss or the company will pay the tab.

Cell Phones and Technology Manners

One of the more challenging and problematic issues regarding manners in business settings revolves around the use of technology, specifically smart phones, tablets, laptops, and other digital devices. As technology develops, determining how to limit their use in business events will become even more important.

In some situations, technology enables a group of people to accomplish tasks that they otherwise would not be able to complete in as efficient a manner. In other cases, technology—particularly the smart phone—interrupts events and destroys the flow of conversation and decision making.

In most cases, the person hosting the meeting determines what is acceptable, technologically, in the meeting. If there is a PowerPoint presentation and the room is darkened—slightly or fully—you should feel free to take notes on the handout, on your own pad of paper, or on a tablet or laptop. If everyone is provided with a laptop or tablet—or asked to bring their own—you should be prepared to participate in that manner.

Mobile phones, however, are a different matter. Most people starting meetings or business meals will say something about not using mobile phones, just like at a concert, movie, or play, but sometimes the person will not say anything. Increasingly, people at business meetings or meals are expected to place their phones on the table to the left of their plate or pad of paper so that everyone can see them. This placement lets people see if they get a message or text and not interrupt the meeting. It also prevents people from leaning back from the table to read their emails and texts while partially participating in the meeting. It is rude to pull out of the meeting this way.

If you do get a call and you need to answer it, simply pick up the phone from the table—having placed it there so you don't have to rummage for it in your pocket, briefcase, or purse—and head to a quiet place where you will not disturb the progress of the meeting or the conversation at the table. When you have finished the call and dealt with its repercussions, return to the table with a short apology—no details needed—and resume your participation.

Good business practice used to mean returning phone calls within the day or twenty-four hours at least; that window has now changed and people expect an instant response. Avoid that expectation by specifying when you will be in a meeting or unavailable and generally by promising your colleagues and customers a careful response, if not an immediate one. Of course, there are always difficult situations and emergencies. If you encounter one, tell the person running the meeting or hosting the meal that you have to address an important matter, and answer the phone while leaving the room. It is exceptionally awkward and rude to interrupt a meeting by taking a call and continuing the conversation in the room.

Answering your phone at a large-scale presentation or reception can be done easily and unobtrusively by leaving the room to take care of your business. There is no one to alert.

Cultural Variations

Today's business people need to acknowledge and address differences among various cultures—both national and regional. For example, the Korean and Chinese custom of using toothpicks at the end of the meal while at the table—so long as your hand covers the activity—is very appropriate, though it would be frowned on in the United States. And people in the northeastern US—especially the Boston–New York–Washington, DC, corridor—want to conduct business with alacrity, which is not true in the other regions of the country, such as the South and the Southwest.

Different cultures have various ways of greeting new acquaintances. Some shake hands, some hug and kiss, and some bow at the other person and expect a similar bow in return. Some cultures avoid touching on greeting, while others use physical contact as part of getting to know the other person and treating them as someone important.

Another difference among cultural groups involves the use of hands for eating. In the United States, people use their hands for a few foods—french fries, hamburgers, and pizza—but in some countries, diners use their hands to eat most foods. Ethiopian, Indian, Mexican, and other cuisines often require diners to eat with their hands. In Asian countries, most diners use chopsticks and would rarely be comfortable using a knife and fork with their food.

Honor the differences in cultures by paying special attention to the ways things are done in environments that are different from yours. Ask questions—in a respectful manner—about what to do. Regardless of the culture, learn in advance the traditions of any group you are visiting so that you can complete your work effectively and not embarrass yourself.

Sexism and Gallantry

Many people are bewildered by the issue of chivalry and sexism. Should I open the door for a woman in a business setting? Am I being sexist if I do? Am I being presumptuous? Should I let a man open the door for me or get me a drink? While the context may alter the appropriateness of your behavior, opening a door is always appreciated—whether you are a man or a woman—especially if the person is older. At a reception or special event, there is nothing wrong with either men or women offering to get a person a drink. Hospitality and graciousness are never out of style and never out of place, whatever one's gender.

If the recipient of your action does not appreciate your effort and refuses the assistance, you have not made any errors. On the contrary, you have shown yourself to be thoughtful, helpful, and supportive. This attitude will only reflect positively on you in business settings. In fact, these little actions showing courtesy and graciousness will distinguish you from others and reflect well on your company or organization. Remember that no one in business has been criticized for knowing and practicing good manners.

Profane language, off-color jokes, sexist comments, and vulgar references do not belong in business settings or anywhere else where good manners are practiced. Such comments and use of language indicate a disregard for the women at the event and for the professionalism and elegance of the setting. Your inability to stifle that language indicates that you have poor manners and no regard for your colleagues.

Of course, your use of language should also reflect equal treatment of men and women. Referring to the opinion of "the little lady" or "the lesser sex" is very rude, bad manners, and a lethal strategy if you want to be taken seriously. At the same time, don't refer to "all us guys" when there are women in the group, unless you mean to exclude the women. Reminding people not to use sexist language is very appropriate.

Do not use profane language or point with food

Spouses and Partners

Your spouse, partner, or date may be invited to an occasional business event, but in most situations, they are not included either due to the structure of the event—there is no real social time—or the confidentiality of the business being discussed. If you want to bring your spouse or partner, or even a date, to a business event, make sure that you ask first and consider the consequences of asking. Spouses and partners may be excluded for good reason. Asking to bring yours indicates your lack of good manners and ignorance of the customs and traditions of your business.

If your partner is invited in advance to a business event, by all means feel free to include that person and prepare him for the event in terms of expected dress, language, and behavior. Remember that his behavior reflects on you. Because partners are invited mostly for social aspects of conferences, trade shows, and conventions, they should be prepared to meet and greet individuals and keep up coherent and interesting conversations. If they are uncomfortable in those settings, it might be better to leave them at home. (For more information, see the **Meeting and Greeting** section in **Chapter 6. Manners in Business Settings** and the **Carrying on Conversations** section of **Chapter 2. Conduct Becoming a Guest**.)

In addition, during the event, your responsibility is to your companion as well as to the purpose of the business event. Knowing that reality ahead of time can help both of you move comfortably through the event and greet the range of people attending. If the social event includes a number of spouses, partners, dates, and friends, the context changes, and most everyone can be comfortable. If you are one of only a few who has a companion, the stress on you and your partner or date can be severe; preparing for it can help both of you. Even sharing this chapter with your spouse, partner, or date can be helpful, especially if she wants to help you with your networking—the major agenda for all business events.

During the event, help your spouse, partner, or date learn the names of your co-workers and other colleagues. Remember to introduce him often and pay attention to what kind of evening he is experiencing. Because the company stories and inside jokes can exclude the person accompanying you, be sure to translate some statements and explain some behaviors.

Leaving the Event

The process of saying good-bye and leaving a business event differs dramatically depending on the type of event. If you have been attending a huge charity event, you need to say good-bye only to your tablemates and whoever invited you to the event. You do not need to find the organizers and thank them, unless you know them personally.

On the other hand, if you have been part of a small dinner party in a private dining room (whether you were being considered for a position or were part of a group vetting others as potential business partners), taking your leave needs to follow the customary pattern of guests leaving first and then individuals in order of ascending rank or importance. The guest leaving first enables the host or organizer to invite his colleagues to share their perceptions of the evening and the people who were being entertained. Sometimes this recap works best in the office, but often the immediacy of the moment and the dynamics of travel schedules lead to a more private and productive discussion at the end of the evening.

The host, or the person organizing the event, will be the last person to leave unless everyone leaves at the same time. This pattern allows the host to make sure that no one has left anything in the dining room and that the bill, service issues, and other aspects of the evening have been handled appropriately and professionally.

For all other events—which fall between these two extremes—leaving is a matter of taking cues from the host or organizer. If he insists that you stay, take the hint that he does not want you to leave. The invitation to stay may be about a chance to continue or pursue a topic of conversation or an issue that did not get resolved earlier. In some cases, the host or organizer may want your comments and feedback on the event. In other cases, the topic may be something else entirely. In any case, staying provides you with a chance to continue working more closely with the host, and you should make every effort to remain and participate actively and effectively. Remember that business events are about business and networking; the invitation to stay provides another occasion for building relationships. Sometimes, though, the invitation is only perfunctory, and you should indicate your desire or need to leave and thank them.

When you do leave, take time to say "thank you" to each of the hosts or event organizers. That way, they know you left and that you showed appreciation for the event. The primary importance of saying thank you is about recognizing and appreciating the care, work, energy, and expense involved in organizing and hosting a business event.

When you return home, remember to send a handwritten thank you note. It makes a real difference in creating a lasting positive impression. In fact, a thank you note can make a difference in getting hired or obtaining business and being remembered—or not. Many candidates for jobs have been ruled out of contention because of poor manners at an event and the lack of a handwritten thank you note afterwards. As Jacqueline Whitmore has written, "A well written note could increase the chance of getting your foot in a company's door or give you an edge over other competitors vying for the same account." Because they are read carefully and often kept—unlike electronic mail—thank you notes make an impression. They are also a magic opportunity to unlock major opportunities. The thank you note can be a key to open new doorways.

CHAPTER 7

Pet Peeves at Dinner Parties

Just as manners run the gamut, people's reactions to poor manners vary widely, too. Some people react strongly to bad manners, which can ruin an evening or event for them. Others are perturbed by certain bad manners but can overlook them. One person's really horrible pet peeve can be another person's mild annoyance. What follows is a range of pet peeves that bother people and advice about how to handle them, whether you are a host or a guest at an event.

Use a fork and knife properly and not in this manner

Poor Eating Habits

People acting like slobs at the dining table can quickly disrupt a dinner party. Watching people slurp their food, lick their fingers, or talk with their mouth full is not a pleasant experience. In fact, some people lose their appetite when confronted with the poor eating habits of their fellow dinner guests or restaurant patrons. The following list of pet peeves indicates a range of activities and behaviors that can impact a perfectly good dinner party in any setting.

Do not start to eat food before others are served and the host indicates it is time to start

Eating before others are served. One of the cardinal rules of good dining involves waiting to make sure that everyone is served before starting to eat. In fact, at a dinner party, each of the guests should wait for the host to start eating—or at least to put the fork or other appropriate utensil on the plate—or invite people to start eating. That way, everyone is served and everyone eats at the same time. In fact, at dinner parties, guests should wait in case the host wants to say grace or invite a guest to say grace. If you see a guest starting to eat, cough loudly to help her notice that no one has started to eat, or ask the host if grace will be said. Engaging the guest in conversation may stop her eating by focusing on the discussion. If you are the host, you can ask individuals to wait until everyone is served. If the guest who starts eating before the host is from a different country or culture, you may want to overlook this lapse of good American manners.

Do not mash, mix, or swirl food on a plate

Playing with food indicates a lack of proper table manners, and you should not do it, even to disguise the fact that you are not eating much of the meal. As a guest, if you see a person playing with his food, ignore it and focus on the conversation. You might try inviting the diner into the conversation with a direct question; changing his focus might interrupt his playing with food. As a host, ignoring it demonstrates your good manners and your interest in making the guest comfortable. If it continues, ask the guest if he would like something different to eat and offer to provide it. It is a way of recognizing the behavior and not demeaning your guest.

Do not show your food

Showing food while chewing, chewing with an open mouth, or spitting while chewing food is poor manners. Chewing food with your mouth open demonstrates a lack of attention to and concern for the other people at the dining table. It also tends to produce spittle and expelled food. Either situation is unpleasant for other guests and should be avoided. If you have difficulty keeping your mouth closed or you tend to talk with your mouth full, simply place your hand in front of your mouth while you are chewing. As a guest, look away in order to avoid drawing attention to the situation and to ensure that you are not repelled by this behavior. As a host, you should ignore the behavior. Although guests should know better, pointing out poor manners will not help the situation and will only make the guest feel uncomfortable.

Speaking with your mouth full is a common display of bad manners. You should finish chewing before responding to the question being asked. It is perfectly reasonable to expect your dinner companions to wait for you to finish what is in your mouth. If you feel you must answer a question when your mouth is full, cover your mouth and speak. Suggest that the person asking a question wait for an answer if the respondent's mouth is full. You can also contribute to the conversation while waiting for the person to finish his food. That way, you keep the conversation going and give the guest time to eat comfortably. Look away if another guest is speaking with a full mouth so you don't draw attention to his bad manners.

Eating rolls improperly bothers many people. Proper manners require that guests take a piece of bread—whether a roll, slice of bread, muffin, or other bread product—from the bread basket and place it on a bread and butter plate. Keep in mind that it is improper to handle all the bread in the basket before taking your piece. You should then break the bread into pieces, one at a time, and then butter each piece—or dip it if using olive oil—and eat just that piece. Buttering all your bread at once and eating the roll in one bite demonstrates a lack of manners. As a guest, ignore this behavior and focus on the conversation at the table. A host should also ignore this behavior, since talking about it only draws attention to the lack of good manners.

Do not lick your fingers after finishing a meal or a dish

Licking your fingers in some countries is part of normal table manners, but it is not acceptable at a dinner party in the United States. If confronted with this situation, guests and hosts should ignore the behavior and focus on the conversation happening at another area of the dining table. Drawing attention to this unsanitary behavior only will make the offending guest uncomfortable and uneasy. If this behavior occurs during cocktails, hand the guest another cocktail napkin, which provides a subtle hint that he does not have to—and should not—use his mouth to clean his fingers. You can also use this situation to indicate the location of the restroom, and invite the guest to wash his hands. If the guest has licked his fingers and then taken food from a bread basket or an hors d'oeuvres plate during cocktails, simply refrain from eating anything from that basket or platter. If the behavior bothers you a great deal, ask the guest not to lick fingers at the dinner table. A more direct approach is to hand the guest an individual hand wipe or package of wet towelettes.

Do not eat off your knife

Eating from a knife is way beyond proper American manners. When a person eats from a knife—and not in British style—there is nothing to say. Just do not watch closely or draw attention to these poor manners. The worst thing you can do is criticize it publicly, since your comments will only make the other person uncomfortable. If the guest comes from a country where this behavior is common, just continue the conversation. If the guest was raised in the United States, he may not know—or want to practice—the basic principles of good manners and, therefore, is someone you may not want to invite to your house in the future.

Putting butter directly on bread should not be done. When eating bread, move the butter to the bread and butter plate; do not butter your bread directly from the butter dish. Most people realize that they should serve themselves a helping of butter from a central serving plate, place it on their bread plate, and then use it to butter their bread or rolls one piece at a time. If you see a guest use the central butter plate to butter her bread directly, ask for the bread and butter plate, take some butter from the central plate, and move it to your bread and butter plate, thereby showing the guest how it should be done. If the behavior continues, ignore it, because a dinner party is not the place to teach manners. As a host, you can request the guest not butter her bread from the central plate.

Slurping or belching at the table while eating food is a mark of poor manners. In the United States, it is not acceptable manners to make noises while eating. Slurping food and belching both make a lot of noise. It does not reflect well on you as a dinner guest, and it can make other people very uncomfortable. If you find yourself in the situation where diners are making a lot of noise while eating, simply ask them to eat a bit more quietly or model eating the dish without making a lot of noise. If someone born or raised in the United States burps at the table, simply say, "Excuse me" for the person, regardless of whether you are a fellow guest or the host. If you are a host and your guest is slurping or belching or otherwise eating his food in a particularly noisy manner, request that he eat more quietly. A second strategy is to model the behavior more vividly so that he gets the hint.

Poor Manners

Guests who don't know the basic rules of good manners at a dinner party annoy plenty of people. They may never have learned them or may have forgotten them if their colleagues or friends don't use them on a regular basis. Here are some breaches of good manners that can cause unhappiness or heartburn at a dinner party.

Leaving a napkin beside the plate during dinner. Most people realize that they should remove their napkin from the table and put it in their lap as soon as they sit down. Unfortunately, some people forget and need to be reminded. Making a show of putting your napkin in your lap can help the person remember. Pointing to her napkin can serve the same purpose. People who keep their napkin on the table and use it to wipe their mouth or fingers and then return it to the table may need a stronger reminder, or a more obvious demonstration, that napkins belong in laps. However, like many instances of poor manners, you should ignore the behavior because drawing attention to it may simply make the individual guest and everyone at the table uncomfortable.

Do not stack your plates or lean your elbows on the table

Placing elbows on the table is appropriate in some European countries, but not in the United States. There is no excuse for putting elbows on the table; doing so demonstrates poor manners in both private dinner party and restaurant settings. If you see this action happen, you can choose to ignore the behavior or say something about it, realizing that mentioning it may make the other person uncomfortable. While this behavior may be common, especially at family dinners, it is bad manners at dinner parties. If you must lean on anything, lean on your forearms, which should be placed only on the edge of the table. As a host, ignore the behavior. This breach of good manners won't destroy the evening, and drawing attention to it may simply make everyone at the table uncomfortable.

Stealing food from another person's plate without their permission offends most people. In some situations—among real foodies—people share food from one another's plates all the time, especially if they are good friends and like to taste different items. If you are a guest, you should ask the person's permission to taste food from their plate, unless, of course, the person is your partner and you do it often. However, at a dinner party, most guests have the same food, so it is not common and should not be practiced. If you are a host and a guest declines an item that you are serving, you can always offer him a small taste, requesting an opinion of the item.

Putting a napkin on the plate instead of on the table at the end of the meal is inappropriate. At the end of a meal, the napkin should be placed on the table to the left of the plate, or left in the chair. It should not be tossed on top of a plate, where it will mingle with food and create a mess for cleanup. It adds more work for the host, and it is an unnecessary and thoughtless blunder. It is also unsanitary. If you are the host, remove the napkin promptly—if you can do so unobtrusively—so that it is not extra work to clean up later. At some dinner parties where guests help clear the table and take dishes to the kitchen for later cleanup, they will clear the plates and then collect the napkins in the kitchen and place them together in a cleanup area or hamper for laundry.

Piling your food on a plate at a buffet shows that you do not understand how a buffet works. It is never appropriate to load your plate. Help yourself to what you want and remember that you can always return to the buffet for more food. As a guest, if you see someone loading his plate, suggest to him—in a friendly manner—that stacking his food in towers may make it hard to eat and easy to spill. You can also remind him that there will be plenty of food, and he can return to the buffet table. As a host, you can make the same comment, which may encourage the guest to take less food on his plate. As a host, you can provide extra plates at the end of the buffet to indicate that there is plenty of food and that you want people to use a fresh plate when they return to the buffet. Or you can provide only small plates, which encourages several visits and discourages piling of food.

Using your fork or spoon to serve yourself from a serving platter shows a lack of knowledge of manners. This habit is not sanitary and should not be tolerated at a dinner party or in any other situation. If you see it happen, avoid the food that has been touched by the spoon or fork and ask the host for another serving utensil, which is a subtle indication that the guest did not use the correct utensil. To avoid this situation as a host, make sure that you provide the correct serving utensil and a sufficient number of serving utensils for each of the dishes on the table. (For more information about serving styles, see the section in **Chapter 4. A Well Set Table**.) If you're not sure which food has been touched by the spoon or fork do not serve yourself any of that food unless you are comfortable with the guest and know him well. As the host, you may want to remove the dish of food that has been touched by the personal spoon or fork and then provide a new serving utensil while removing the already touched food, if possible, before returning it to the table. You may also want to take this opportunity to remind the guest to use only serving utensils when bringing food from a serving dish to her plate.

Restaurant Behavior

There are many actions taken in restaurants that bother other guests. Some of them have become prevalent only recently, and others have been frustrating examples of poor manners for a long time. The following list ranges from the relatively new to classic bad manners.

Ordering food from a guidebook bothers many people when they see it. One of the unfortunate consequences of the prevalence of online restaurant reviews is the tendency of some diners to use them in deciding where to go for dinner and what to order when they arrive. You may have seen people reading a review from a restaurant review site while scanning the menu to find the exact item that the reviewer mentioned, a behavior that bothers restaurateurs and a few other guests. If a restaurant is good, why not try any menu item? If your dining companions operate this way, simply ask them to consider the range of quality items on the menu and point out that dishes may have changed since the review was posted. If they persist in demanding the menu item in the review, you may decide not to join them for dinner in a restaurant in the future. Simply smile and leave the challenge of handling them to your server.

Do not wear a baseball cap at a nice restaurant

Wearing a hat is rude. Hats do not belong on male restaurant patrons in nice restaurants. Eating outdoors can be a reason to wear a hat to provide some cover and protection from the sun. However, you don't need to advertise your favorite team or company by wearing a baseball cap in a fine dining restaurant. If a guest comes to the table wearing a hat, simply ask him to remove it during dinner. You can say, "Please take your hat off so that I can see your face, which is much better looking than your hat," or, "I cannot see you smile or participate in the conversation when you wear that hat. Please take it off for me." If the guest persists in wearing the hat throughout dinner, it indicates that he has no manners and will not be someone you want to meet at a white tablecloth restaurant again. Hats worn by women in elegant settings should also be removed while at the table.

Do not text while at the table at a dinner party

Emailing, texting, or using a smartphone, tablet, or other device is not appropriate during a dinner with others. It detracts from the attention that should be paid to other people and gets in the way of appreciating the food and beverages. It is rude to your host and to the other guests. If you need to text someone, simply excuse yourself from the table. If it is not necessary, just stop the behavior and pay attention to your restaurant companions. As a guest or host, you can say to those who are texting, "I wish you would not do that at the table. I would rather talk with you than watch you play with your machine." You should make the comment in a friendly and easy conversational manner. There is no reason to use an angry, critical, or condescending tone of voice. Then resume the conversation you were having.

Do not talk on cell phones

Multiple guests talking on their cell phones at the same time is becoming increasingly common and not fun to watch unless you have a strange sense of humor. It is ironic to find two people dining together with each of them on their mobile devices, not paying attention to the other. If a diner starts to pick up her cell phone during dinner, ask her not to use it and invite her to have a conversation. If she persists, focus your attention on other people at the table and ignore her rude behavior. As a last resort, pick up your cell phone and call or text the diner to say that you would like to talk in person. There are electronic devices and applications you can add to your mobile device that block reception in the immediate area of your device; perhaps using one of them might make the point, and your fellow diners may not know why they cannot receive any messages. Good manners suggest checking on possible urgent or emergency calls before using such a device.

Showing pictures from smartphones at the table interrupts conversation and destroys the sense of community at dinner. Some people love their pictures and take advantage of any opportunity to share those pictures, regardless of your interest or the value of the pictures to others at the table. While some people are excited to see them, most people are not, and it is inappropriate behavior at a dinner party. It draws attention away from the conversation, makes the topic all about the individual showing pictures, and lets only one person at a time see the pictures. (If you need to show pictures of a child, grandchild, or new acquisition, use the time during cocktails instead.) As a guest, if you are offered the pictures, indicate that you would like to see them at another time. Then ask the person who wants to show the pictures a question in the hopes that the topic of conversation will move forward. If you see her sharing pictures and pushing them on everyone, invite her to share the pictures later. Say, "Thank you for your willingness to show us your pictures, but I would rather see them at another time," or, "I am sure they are lovely pictures, but we don't have a chance to visit enough so let's talk to each other," and resume the conversation.

Domineering talking from a nearby table can ruin an evening out. There is nothing more frustrating than going to a nice restaurant, looking forward to visiting with family, friends, or colleagues, and finding that the people at the next table talk so loud that you cannot hear yourself, much less the conversation at your table. Some restaurants are designed with acoustical dynamics in mind, but some are echo chambers, and loud people nearby only make it worse. To address this situation, you can get up, walk over to the neighboring table, and ask them politely if they could speak a little more quietly so that you and your friends could hear your own conversation. If this strategy does not work or you are uncomfortable doing it, ask your server—or the restaurant manager—to intervene on your behalf. Since the restaurant staff members want you to be happy, they will be glad to speak to the guests at the other table. Their requests are often more successful.

Do not load your plate with too much food

Loading food on a plate or making towers of food from a buffet shows ignorance of buffet etiquette. In some restaurants, a buffet is offered for the first course, and sometimes the entire meal is served in that manner. Remember that you can return to the buffet as many times as you want (and use a clean plate each time); there is no need to load your plate and create an unappetizing and potentially unsafe pile of food. If you see someone in your dinner party doing it, suggest that he can return to the buffet as many times as he wants and remind him that he should take a fresh plate each time. If he does not want to hear your message, simply ignore him and return to your table. You are not likely to make a difference in his behavior.

Asking for salt or pepper without tasting the food indicates a lack of regard for the chef. Some guests—at a restaurant or a dinner party—start the meal by putting salt and pepper on their food without even looking at or tasting the food. Many cooks regard this practice as an implicit criticism of their food and consider it rude. In fact, many chefs do not place salt and pepper on dining tables so that people are forced to taste the food first. Unfortunately, some restaurants have adopted the practice of offering pepper for every course as a way of showing attention before a guest has tasted the food. If you can, refrain from accepting the fresh ground pepper until you have tasted the food. In some business settings, using salt and pepper before tasting the food will indicate that you rush to judgment, and, therefore, you might not get the position or appointment that you want.

Not sharing food at a Chinese restaurant when everyone ordered platters expecting to share the items can frustrate your dinner companions. Although it is very common to select dishes to share when dining at a Chinese restaurant, some people do not like to share their food at all. If you think that your dining companions may not be the type to share, raise the issue as part of the conversation when selecting what to order. If they do not want to share and indicate that fact before the food comes, you are prepared and can order separate food items accordingly. If your dining companions do not say that they don't want to share, you are going to be caught in an awkward situation when you start to help yourself to platters that they ordered. Simply apologize and remember to order differently next time. Or consider whether you want to dine with them at a Chinese restaurant next time.

Do not take pictures of food at the table

Practicing food pornography (taking pictures of all the food with a smartphone) can destroy an evening. (The phrase "food pornography" describes people for whom the picture taking is addictive and more important than enjoying the meal and your company.) While taking pictures of food has become a very popular hobby, sitting at a restaurant while your dinner companion takes pictures of all the items on the table can be a very uncomfortable situation for you and other restaurant patrons. Some people even take pictures of the breadbasket or the table setting! If this practice makes you uncomfortable, simply request that she not take any pictures during dinner and invite her to talk about the food so that she can remember it.

Refusing to leave a decent tip indicates a lack of appreciation for the work of the staff in a restaurant. Ironically, some of the people who are most demanding about service are the least generous with tips. Tips are one of the ways that you share your appreciation for the hard work of your server and the other people who helped make your dinner special. Increasingly, restaurants are providing information about how much a tip would be if it were 10 percent, 15 percent, or 20 percent of the bill, with some of them listing 18 percent. These guidelines make it easier to calculate a tip at the end of a meal. If you are part of a large party, most restaurants automatically calculate an 18-to-20-percent service charge and add it to the bill because groups do not have a good reputation for tipping appropriately. If part of your group does not want to leave a tip, start a conversation about all the things the wait staff did to make the evening special. Often, that discussion will lead them to change their behavior and leave an appropriate amount. If this strategy does not work and you appreciated the service, you may decide to add extra money yourself.

Loud noise can destroy a dinner party. When the sound from background music disturbs you, ask your server if there is a way to turn down—or otherwise modify—the volume of the music. Mention that it is making it difficult to carry on a conversation or hear your dining partners and that you came to this restaurant for a meal and conversation. Normally, the staff will make the changes you request, as they want you to enjoy your experience in the restaurant. Occasionally, you may need to make the request several times. If the sound situation does not improve, request moving to another seat where the sound might be less intrusive.

Finding yourself too cold or too hot in the restaurant can ruin an evening. Sometimes, the location of a table may mean that you are too hot or too cold during a meal. Ask your server to change the temperature and indicate that you may not be alone; there may be others in the restaurant who are similarly uncomfortable. If the temperature cannot be adjusted, request a change in table location so that you can enjoy the meal.

Eating before everyone is served is basic bad manners. Having good manners means waiting for everyone to be served a course before starting to eat. At a restaurant where some diners may have ordered a first course and others have not, guests may eat the first course after everyone who ordered that course is served. You should remember who did and did not order that course; asking is very appropriate. However, when everyone has ordered a course, refrain from beginning to eat the food on your plate until everyone has a plate in front of them. Of course, if a guest was served the wrong food or it was prepared incorrectly or differently than ordered, then you can begin to eat without that person. (Since that person was technically served a plate and had to send it back, you are not really waiting for him to be served. He already was.)

Splitting a bill unevenly can frustrate your dinner companions. Most colleagues, friends, and family members who go out to eat together expect to share the cost of the meal (plus tax and tip) equally. In that case, ask one person to be the treasurer and calculate the bill. Some people give their server individual credit cards and ask her to divide the bill equally according to the number of credit cards. When dividing it among couples, the process is easy. If there are single people and couples in the dinner party, ask your server to charge some credit cards twice as much as others (for couples) or ask couples to use two different credit cards to make it easier on the server. If people do not want to split the cost evenly—because someone is on a limited diet and will not eat much or if someone else wants to order expensive wine and treat everyone to it—the situation can be awkward for everyone involved. If people want to pay individually, common courtesy dictates that you ask the server, at the beginning of the meal before ordering, if it is possible to have separate checks. Most servers are skilled in dividing the bill according to your instructions.

Requesting doggie bags for leftovers should not be done in fine dining restaurants. There are times in casual or family-oriented restaurants when the entrée contains a lot of food and a restaurant will offer to wrap uneaten food to take home. That activity often makes sense. However, when a guest asks other people to give her their food to take home, it is poor manners. If it bothers you, simply decline to share your food and graciously indicate that you do not want to take it home yourself. If the guest is disturbed by your refusal, overlook the criticism or frustration and continue the conversation. There is one exception: going to a restaurant with the intention of ordering a meal to bring home to a person who is sick or unable to be present at the restaurant (although invited). In that case, give the server the order when you order your own food, and the staff will bring it to you packaged to carry when you leave. Otherwise, avoid asking for to-go bags or "doggie" bags of food.

Serving Issues in Restaurants

There are many things that wait staff and servers do that can create a wonderful evening or bring frustration to restaurant patrons and ruin a dining experience. Here is what servers or other restaurant staff members do to detract from an otherwise beautiful evening.

Addressing restaurant patrons in an informal manner. "Darling," "Sweetie," "Hon," "Guys," "Babe," or "Dude" at a white tablecloth restaurant can be very frustrating to people who expect to be addressed more formally. The wait staff should refer to their guests as "Sir" or "Ma'am," because these titles indicate respect, not a false and inappropriate familiarity. If you find the wait staff calling you by inappropriate names, simply tell them that you do not appreciate this way of being addressed. You can provide them with language you want them to use, but you do not have to do so. Indicate that you do not want familiar forms of address. However, if you are at a diner or fast-food restaurant or dining in a restaurant located in the South, you may find yourself addressed in this informal manner. In that case, just be patient, enjoy the terms of endearment, and do not complain. While calling restaurant patrons "Honey," "Dude," "Dearie," "Sweetie," and "Hon" may be condescending or inappropriate (depending on the type of restaurant), it may be part of the way in which the service staff was trained.

Servers introducing themselves using their first names as a way to start the conversation with people at a dinner table is a common pet peeve. If you are offended by the style and conversational attitude of your server, simply state that fact to your server and expect him to adapt. You are spending the money and deserve to be treated in a manner that is comfortable to you.

Lingering over the table or chatting up diners by wait staff offends many restaurant patrons. Paying lots of attention to you and the other people at your table or lingering over the table unnecessarily makes many guests uncomfortable. It limits the conversation because the group does not feel it has any privacy. Unfortunately, servers who are not fully occupied by the demands of their tables can—and often do—pay you much more attention than you want or are comfortable with. In this situation, say that you wish to receive a bit less attention and ask for some space. In small restaurants where there are few restaurant patrons, this situation can be difficult to manage. However, asking for privacy and less attention is still very appropriate and perfectly good manners.

Serving food too early should not be done in a decent restaurant. One of the pleasures of eating at a restaurant is the chance to linger over a cocktail or other before-dinner drink. Unfortunately, some servers pay little to no attention to your desires about the timing of the meal. They do not ask nor do they pay attention and often bring you food when you are not yet prepared to eat it. The solution to this dilemma is to mention, at the first interaction with the server, that you want to eat a slow and leisurely dinner and you want to order the courses in turn. This information may be necessary because most wait staff are trained to obtain orders and ensure that courses come out promptly.

Ignoring or not noticing dirty flatware shows a lack of attention to table management. The flatware in a restaurant should be well washed and polished (especially in a white tablecloth restaurant). If it's dirty, ask the server to provide you with a new set of flatware. If the server does not return promptly with fresh silverware and your fellow guests already have their food and have started eating, help yourself to the flatware that you need at a side stand.

Clearing plates from the table when someone is still eating is an indication that staff members have not learned proper service techniques. If your server starts to clear plates while your dining companions are midmeal, tell him that you would prefer to let everyone eat their full course before any of the plates are removed. Say, "Please leave the plates until we are all finished." In some restaurants, this practice is encouraged to provide more room at the table. If you cannot stop the server from removing plates and she has already taken one, say, "We would rather wait until everyone is finished before you remove any more plates." If you have been practicing the rule of placing your knife and fork at four o'clock on the plate only when you are finished, and you have your utensils at a different location on the plate, your server should realize that you are not yet done.

Do not auction off food

Forgetting who ordered which dish—and auctioning off food as a result—is not appropriate at a fine dining restaurant. This practice is acceptable at diners and similar informal eating establishments where there is no record of who ordered which dish, or where wait staff persons carry many plates to a table they have not waited upon. However, auctioning food at a white tablecloth or family-style restaurant indicates that the restaurant does not know how to record who ordered what item or how to serve its guests in an appropriate fashion. Tell the server to put the plates down and ask the people at your table which is theirs. If the server doesn't agree, offer to take the plates and distribute them yourself. While this behavior may be considered aggressive, it can make a point with the server and facilitate what could otherwise be a mess and a disruption of the conversation at the table. If this disorganized behavior does not change and it offends you, then you know not to return to this restaurant.

Yelling at staff in public by restaurant owners or managers should not happen. Raising one's voice at anyone in a restaurant, no matter what level, should not be tolerated. If you hear the yelling and it disturbs you, wave the wait staff person over and mention it. If the manager or owner is doing the yelling, excuse yourself from the table and go talk to that person. There is no excuse for anyone—guest or staff member—treating staff in that manner. Try to move to a quiet corner so that you can talk undisturbed and mention that your dinner is being ruined. You can say, "Our dinner is being disturbed by the noise in this restaurant. Is there any way you can moderate the volume so that we can enjoy our dinner?" That strategy allows the manager an opportunity to correct the problem and does not lay the blame on the person directly.

Being abandoned by wait staff when trying to pay the bill or being presented with the bill too early frustrates many restaurant patrons. The best restaurant waiters remain attentive to the table all evening long, but sometimes wait staff do not realize that the most lasting impression is often the most recent one, and they seem to ignore the table after serving the coffee. On the other hand, some servers provide you with the bill when they serve the coffee, seeming to encourage you to leave as soon as you can. Either situation is frustrating. You can address the first situation by getting up and looking for your server in order to obtain the bill or to provide the server with your credit card. In the second situation, ask your server if there is an immediate need for the table and act accordingly. Even if the bill is on the table, you should feel comfortable lingering as long as you want unless you see a crowd of people waiting for a table.

Host and Hostess Issues

Even hosts can aggravate their guests. Good hosts are very attentive to the needs of their guests and will try to make them comfortable to ensure that the evening is a success. However, he may go beyond what puts people at ease and do things that are frustrating. The following topics include some of those behaviors.

Filling your glass of wine all the time is the mark of a hospitable host, but it frustrates some dinner guests. Some hosts are so quick to refill glasses of wine that you can't measure your intake of the beverage. Finding your wine glass always full tends to encourage you to drink more. If you do not want more wine, place your hand over your glass or tell the host that you have had enough wine for now. As a host, pay attention to the amount of wine that your guests are drinking and do not automatically refill glasses that are being emptied slowly. People who are drinking wine more quickly will appreciate a refill; others may not. You can also pass a bottle around the table, thereby giving each guest the opportunity to refill—or decline to refill—the glass.

Leaving the table to answer the telephone during a dinner party is rude (though it makes sense in unusual or emergency situations). As a guest, continue the conversation with your fellow dinner guests if your host has left the table. There is nothing that you can do. As a host, refrain from answering calls—unless you are expecting an important or emergency call—because it communicates the notion that any call is more important than the people you have invited for dinner. If you are expecting an urgent call, tell your guests that you may need to check the phone if it rings.

Providing no indication that the dinner party is over and it is time to go home before the conversation dies can pose a problem for dinner guests. Some hosts are reluctant to end a wonderful evening, others do not know how to do it, and even more like to extend the evening when they are enjoying themselves. As a guest, you have the right to leave at any appropriate time after dinner has concluded. (For more information, see the section **Ending the Evening** in **Chapter 2. Conduct Becoming a Guest** or the section **Encouraging Guests to Leave** in **Chapter 3. Conduct Becoming a Host**.) If the host looks tired or if you want to leave, simply tell the host that you must go. You can describe a responsibility you have the next morning, or just focus on thanking them for a wonderful evening, and say that it is time to leave. This way you invite others to say their thank-yous and good-byes as well. Remember that you have not broken up the evening; you are simply leaving yourself. Other guests can make their own decisions. If you feel, however, that the host does not know how to end the evening, say something like, "It has been a wonderful evening, and I am sure we all have enjoyed it, but all good things must come to an end. Thank you for a wonderful time." This type of statement may encourage others to leave.

Serving inappropriate food for the dietary requirements of guests shows a lack of concern for dinner guests. Given the increasing number of special diets and the growing number of people who cannot eat a particular food for allergic, dietary, or religious reasons, it is important to provide food appropriate for all your guests. However, some hosts seem oblivious to this reality. If you find yourself in that situation and are served food that you cannot eat, do not take any of that dish if it is passed to you, or request only a small portion if you are being served. Simply do not eat it; you can leave it there or move it around the plate at some point to look like you tasted it. Depending on the situation, you can be honest with your host and explain that you cannot eat certain foods but are happy to eat more salad, bread, or food that you can digest. Most hosts appreciate knowing about dietary requirements and allergic reactions ahead of time. Next time, inform your host at the time you accept the invitation or, at a minimum, sometime before the event.

Conversational Gaffes

The primary purpose of a dinner party—whether at a private home, club, restaurant, or other location—is to provide the pleasures of good company and good conversation, so poor manners in conversation can be very frustrating and daunting to address. They can also destroy the evening. Rude or obnoxiously critical remarks that do not respect everyone at a table can turn a dinner party into an unpleasant experience and should be avoided at all times.

Dominating the conversation during dinner can ruin a dinner party. Having to listen to a person who takes over dinner conversation—often talking loudly and assertively to ensure that everyone can hear and must listen—can be a frustrating experience. No one should control the talk at the table. As a guest, insert your comment into the conversation and invite someone else to share an opinion, thereby expanding the number of people who are talking. If you are the host or hostess, play the same role to divert the conversation to include other people. You can also resume control over the conversation by indicating that the topic has been discussed enough and suggest a new topic. You can also ask the person dominating the conversation to allow others to have their say.

Making jokes about ethnic, religious, or sexual orientation minorities is inappropriate in any setting and especially insensitive at a dinner party. It makes for an icy evening. If a guest makes such remarks, indicate your displeasure and ask her to refrain from making derogatory comments. That request should stop her and other guests from making such statements. As a host, declare that such remarks have no place around your dining table, and thank your guests from refraining from making such intolerant and inconsiderate statements now and in the future.

Asking questions that are too personal can embarrass many dinner guests. When confronted with a personal question that makes you uncomfortable, say that you do not want to answer it or find a friendly way to say that the question is too personal. You could also divert the questioner by saying, "It is a long story, and there is not enough time tonight," "We need a bottle of wine and some time alone for that conversation," or, "What an interesting question. Maybe everyone would like to answer that question." To keep the conversation going, ask the person who asked you the question to start with his answer.

Inappropriate Personal Grooming

Although most people realize that the dining room table is not the place to apply makeup, blow their nose, pick their teeth, comb their hair, or otherwise engage in very personal behaviors, many people continue to demonstrate that they do not know any better. Perhaps one of the most unfortunate situations is sitting beside someone who practices personal hygiene at the dining room table. This person should be encouraged to stop and pursue that activity elsewhere. However, some people need to be reminded about what is appropriate and what is not at a dining table.

Do not refresh your makeup in front of others at the table

Applying lipstick, eyeliner, and powder at the table is rude. There is no valid reason to apply makeup at a dining room table or in a public setting. If you need to add makeup or refresh your makeup during dinner, excuse yourself from the table and go to the restroom, where you can apply or fix your makeup in private. If you see someone starting to apply makeup at the table, ask her, politely, to leave the table to apply or repair her makeup and indicate that it bothers you personally. She may not realize that it makes others uncomfortable and is the wrong location.

Do not blow your nose at the table

Blowing your nose at the table should not be tolerated. This habit is noisy, unclean, and disruptive. If you need to blow your nose, excuse yourself from the table, walk to another room—the restroom is best—and blow your nose there. After blowing your nose, be sure to wash your hands. When finished, return to the table. If you have an oncoming sneeze that does not allow you sufficient time to leave the table, turn your head away from the table and sneeze into a handkerchief, tissue, your sleeve, or—if there is no other option—your napkin. If you have a cold, make sure to bring tissues or several clean handkerchiefs. If you need to continue sneezing, leave the table and blow your nose in the next room or the bathroom. As a host, it is best to ignore this behavior unless it gets in the way of the pleasures of the evening.

Coughing without covering your mouth at the table can ruin the health of dinner companions and should be avoided. Coughing without covering your mouth is a way of spreading your cold or other condition to fellow guests. When you can, refrain from coughing and take appropriate medications before arriving for the dinner party. However, if you cannot control the cough, turn away from the table and cover your mouth with a tissue or handkerchief. If you have no other option, use your napkin or sleeve in order to prevent spreading any germs. If a guest continues to cough, you can ask him to cough in another room. As a host, ignore this behavior unless it gets in the way of the pleasures of the evening, in which case you must address it directly.

Behavior of Children

Many guests are uncomfortable watching or being forced to deal with children in restaurant settings. While most children who are taken to white tablecloth restaurants are well behaved and have been raised to know what to do at a dining table, there are exceptions. Misbehaving children can be very frustrating to restaurant patrons who expect to enjoy the company of their friends, good conversation, fine food, and accompanying beverages. They are paying for a quiet atmosphere. Children who act out a lot belong in family-friendly restaurants.

When children make noises, scream, or cry in the restaurant, their behavior often ruins the experience for other diners. If you find yourself burdened with noisy or screaming children, try to ignore them at first. However, if the behavior continues, you have every right to ask the parents to get their children to lower their voices in deference to others in the restaurant. If a friendly request does not yield the results you want, mention the noise to your server or the manager of the restaurant.

Children should not stand or climb on chairs or booths in restaurants. It is dangerous and bad manners. If you see a young child standing or climbing on a chair, move quickly to get him or her to climb down. It is not safe for the child, other people nearby, or the furniture. The first priority should be to protect the child from danger. Because the main concern is safety, you should feel comfortable speaking to the parent or adult accompanying the child about the behavior, even if some parents may not appreciate your intervention. If the child is old enough, you can mention your safety concerns to the child, but note that many parents do not like strangers speaking to their child. If you are unsuccessful in obtaining a change in behavior, speak to your server or the restaurant manager.

Walking or running around a restaurant is unsafe and inappropriate. In a family restaurant, most patrons expect that children will get up and walk around. The restaurant may provide a special playground area for the kids, which increases their interest in going there. If you are in a family restaurant and children moving around bother you, you have made a poor choice of where to eat. Next time, investigate restaurants a bit more carefully. For the moment, make peace with the children and their behavior. At a fancy, white tablecloth restaurant, allowing a child to move among tables is inappropriate, and you have a right to say something to your server or the parents.

Scolding children in a restaurant can become an unpleasant situation for diners who are not family. If the parental behavior bothers you, try to ignore it, and pay extra attention to the conversation at your table. However, if it persists and remains difficult to ignore, speak to the parent nicely and then to your server or the restaurant manager. (Keep in mind that speaking to the parent directly may trigger defensive behavior and may only make the situation much worse.)

Throwing a ball at the table should not happen in a restaurant or home setting. There is never a good time or a reason to toss a ball at another person sitting at a dinner table. It can be dangerous to people, china, crystal, and other valuables at the table. If you find that happening in a restaurant setting, speak to the parent; if that action does not change the situation, ask the server or manager to stop the inappropriate and unsafe behavior. Standing up and excusing yourself from the table is also a successful way to avoid the ball coming your way. When it has stopped, return to your able and resume the conversation and your meal.

CHAPTER 8

Special Situations: Political Events, Dating Manners, and Very Formal Settings

Good manners are good manners, no matter the situation. You can't go wrong if you follow basic etiquette wherever you are. However, working with a public servant or hosting a public servant adds another challenge to remembering or displaying proper manners, as do dating situations and very formal dinners.

Manners for Public Servants and Elected Officials

Manners for public servants and elected or appointed officials are very similar to manners in business situations. Issues such as meeting and greeting, learning names, acting graciously, and networking are handled in the same manner. (For more information, see those sections in **Chapter 6. Manners in Business Settings**.) However, there are significant variations in eating and drinking, dress codes, and methods of leaving the event. If a public servant or elected official is attending dinner at a friend's house as a private person, all the information about being a guest is relevant. (See **Chapter 3. Conduct Becoming a Guest**.) But being in public at events that are designed for networking, celebrating, vote getting, organizing, fund-raising, or information gathering purposes demands a different range of behaviors because the situations are so public.

As many public servants and elected officials will assure you, they are not immune from—and should not be immune from—practicing basic good manners in every situation. They must carry themselves in a manner befitting the office that they hold. However, they are often more subject to public scrutiny, and people notice what they do very closely. Therefore, public servants, elected persons, and appointed officials—and anyone who wants to make a positive impression on a group—have to be superb examples of good manners. They have to remember that they represent their office at all times, regardless of the context. Public servants have to meet and greet people warmly and intentionally, showing their constituents that they care, even if the interchange is only for a short period of time. They have to remember names or, at least, faces. They have to be gracious at all times and in all situations, and they need to listen to other people's causes and needs instead of always focusing on their own agendas. Basically, they need to pay attention to all the people at an event, often an exhausting task, but a critical one. A public servant faces the additional challenge of attending events where the attendees know his name and often expect that he knows them.

As a public servant, shake everyone's hand

As a public servant, meet everyone you can

Since public servants attend a larger number—and often a broader array—of events than most people, they focus on the purpose of each event, paying special attention to the organizer and showing real appreciation to the attendees, especially those who have been generous with their financial support. However, these events—often large in scale and typically designed to make connections and raise funds—have a different dynamic from that of dinner parties. The public servant is not expected to bring a hostess gift, nor is he expected to play the same role a regular guest would—such as helping the host make the event a success. Instead, she is expected to visit with as many people as possible, showing them that they are the most important person in the room at that moment, and to be courteous with everyone's time. She needs to have the ability to conduct short and meaningful conversations and sound like she's never had that conversation before.

Eating food at these events is secondary to meeting and greeting people. Therefore, public servants and elected officials typically eat beforehand or arrange to have meals after the event because:

- Food is usually not served in a timely manner for public servants who must attend two or three functions—if not more—in a single part of a day: morning, lunch, afternoon, or evening. There is no time for them to eat if they are squeezing several events into one meal period.
- Public servants attend events to meet and greet individuals; they do not want to spend their time eating. There is never enough time to meet and greet all the people they want to contact.
- If there is political capital to be earned by eating someone's favorite pie, hot dog, or other food, the person may eat a small bite, but he tends to avoid

eating more than that at events. He especially avoids food that may be difficult to digest.

- Public servants try not to consume meals when on a dais or other raised platform. This is a preventative measure in case they are called upon to speak and their mouth is full, and also to protect against soiling their outfits.
- In general, they don't eat in public because some food may interfere with their dietary limitations, and they don't have time to get sick from food that may not agree with them.

Public servants rarely consume alcoholic beverages at these events since they do not want—for obvious reasons—pictures of them with drinks in their hand, especially if there are news reporters or photographers present. They also need to be able to focus and keep their wits about them at all times. A public servant who has been drinking does not make a great impression. In fact, it creates the wrong image.

Like business people at business events, public servants tend to drink a lot of water or other nonalcoholic beverages so they can stay focused and make their case effectively to any audience. Therefore, if you are hosting someone at a political event, you may want to have extra bottles of water or other beverages for them.

As a public servant or elected official, use a range of handshake strategies

Because public servants and elected officials meet and greet so many people, many of them have developed a series of handshaking strategies to show engagement and contact. One is the firm and steady handshake while looking a person in the eye—even if only for a fleeting moment. Another is the two-handed handshake in which the person feels the contact of both hands, which often makes the receiver feel special. More refined strategies include the half-nelson—purportedly named after Nelson Rockefeller—which involves holding the shoulder of the person being greeted. This maneuver indicates even more connection. The highest level of handshake intimacy is the full nelson, in which the public servant puts his or her arm around the shoulder of the other person while holding that person's hand. It is just short of a hug. It indicates the importance of the person to the public servant.

Public servants and elected officials are role models, and their behavior is on display at their public events. They are expected to be cordial to their political opponents and detractors, although the acrimony in political campaigns makes that task increasingly difficult. As one elected official said, "The political environment today makes it very hard to have good manners—to be polite, to be gracious, and to be honest—during campaigns." They also must watch their use of language and humor, since their words can be taken out of context and used against them, especially in negative campaign advertisements. As another elected official said, "You cannot allow circumstances to dictate your behavior; your behavior must always be stellar." As a result, they are practiced at ignoring the lack of respect they may be shown in various situations.

Since many public servants and elected officials travel with staff, they must be careful how they talk to and treat their assistants as well as other people at the event. The officials must always monitor what they say and how they say it. They know they should not say or do anything that they do not want to see on the front page of a newspaper. Others have mentioned the grandparent guideline—don't do anything that you don't want your parents or grandparents to know about—which represents a friendly reminder for all public behavior.

They—and you if you are hosting them—must be gracious at all times, even if they need to adopt different manners in different situations. In fact, most public servants—both candidates and those in office—are excellent at sensing local variations of manners and adjusting to them. In some areas, a hug is very inappropriate; in other events and groups, humor or references to local events is expected. Providing information about local mores is very helpful if you are hosting them.

Since public servants meet and greet people constantly, they know how to read name tags quickly, ask for introductions skillfully, and use names regularly to help them—and everyone around them—remember names more easily. Their assistants, organizers, and hosts can help with names, but the challenge of remembering names and using them promptly is up to them.

As a public servant, pose for photographs as a way of honoring people

Candidates and elected officials tend to circulate around tables at events and shake hands with as many people as they can, often exchanging stories and pleasantries. They also often trade business cards or offer to pose for a photograph taken with their constituents. These photographs are then sent to their constituents with a short note thanking them for their support.

Public servants are good at thanking people both publicly and privately. They publicly thank hosts, regardless of how helpful they actually were. Good public servants and elected officials—and sometimes their staff—also send written thank you notes, often enclosing photos from the event. On occasion they may send gifts to acknowledge extraordinary hospitality. They may also send quick email notes—rather than handwritten notes—to show appreciation for having met a person and to establish a future connection.

Hosting Public Servants

Hosting public servants can be challenging because they operate on tight schedules, often filling their day with many meetings and events, and their schedules constantly change due to circumstances mostly beyond their control. Some can become entranced with their position and forget the simple human courtesies toward their assistants, handlers, and hosts. You can control some aspects of hosting a public servant, but not all.

If you are hosting or escorting a public servant—whether seeking office or in office— remember that his goal is to connect with the people who attend. Therefore, help him make contact with as many people as possible and in a way that makes them feel heard or recognized. If the event includes people sitting at tables, help him circulate around the room and meet everyone sitting down (while trying to keep him on schedule).

As a public servant, try to greet as many people as possible

When planning an event you will host for a public servant, you need to consider the following:

- What type of activity will it be?
- What is the purpose of the event for the public servant? How can that best be served?

- Will the public servant speak, and does she need a podium or a raised platform?
- Will she need a public address system?
- Will she need special lighting or a spotlight?
- Does the audience expect a speech? Some questions and answers?
- Will the audience want a chance to shake her hand?
- What will the seating arrangements be?
- What is the dress code?
- Will a meal be served? If so, are you planning a stand-up reception or will people sit at tables?
- Should the press be invited?
- Does the official want photos to be taken?

If, however, you are organizing a private meal with a public servant, you need to follow general hosting manners and make a few additional arrangements. Be sure to exchange cell phone numbers with all members of the group so that if anyone is running late, he can communicate that delay. Make this exchange when reviewing the arrangements in order to allow for the many schedule changes and transportation challenges that public servants face. Confirm arrangements the day before the meeting. The official's plans can change between the time you planned the meal and the day it is scheduled to happen.

Dating and Manners

Dating often means eating meals together, and table manners can make a big difference in the impression that you make on your date for the evening. In fact, for some potential partners, bad manners can be a deal-breaker.

Because you are on a date to find out more about the other person, or to enjoy your partner's company, remember that the first rule of dating manners involves honesty and graciousness. If you invited the other person, tell him what the evening will be like so he doesn't show up underdressed or overdressed for the restaurant you've chosen. If you are running late for the date, let the other person know. In transit, be gracious and open the door. At the restaurant, if your date says something wrong or incorrect, don't criticize it or correct it except in a positive and encouraging manner. If you're asked a question, answer honestly. In short, be genuine and treat your date with dignity throughout the evening.

The second principle of dating manners involves focusing on the comfort and care of your date, whether you are the person asked out on the date or the person who did the asking. In contemporary circles, dating involves both people taking responsibility for the success of the evening. That can mean either person inviting the other, sharing the bill for the dinner and other activities, and ensuring that the other person enjoys herself. If you know more about the cocktails, wine, menu items, or restaurant operation, share your knowledge. If you are unfamiliar with menu items, feel free to ask about them. Traditionally, when one person invites another out on a date, that person expects to pay. If, however, the person simply initiates the conversation about getting together, it has become increasingly common to share the bill. Since these behaviors are changing among younger generations, it is important to decide who pays. If your date is paying the bill, ask her what she's ordering, or how many courses, so that you can select accordingly.

Maintaining interest in the other person and managing conversation is the third principle of good manners when dating. Start with easy topics and move to more complex or personal topics as the evening progresses and both of you become more comfortable. If the evening does not seem to be going well, remain focused on superficial topics and refrain from personal questions or answers. If you've already had several dates, ask about your companion's day or week to show interest in his daily life. Then you can proceed to more intense subjects depending on the answers to the first few questions. You can always ask the other person's opinions and advice to establish a greater connection and show the other person that you value his insights.

Complimenting your date is good manners as long as you do it honestly. Offering effusive compliments that do not match the situation is superficial and dishonest. If in doubt, avoid a compliment and focus on the conversation, the meal, and other topics where you can be genuine and treat the person with dignity. If you get a compliment, say, "Thank you," return the compliment, and steer the conversation to another topic rather than waiting for another one.

At the end of the evening, say, "Thank you" and show that you appreciated the evening in a genuine and honest way. You don't need to do anything you don't wish to do, and you don't "owe" your date anything. The purpose of the date was to get to know each other better and enjoy an evening out. What happens after the dinner is for the two of you to decide.

Very Formal Dinners

On a rare occasion, you may be invited to a very formal dinner where guests are expected to wear black tie and tails, white tie and tails, a tuxedo, and long formal gowns. No matter what the circumstances, the basic principles of good manners hold.

Upon arriving at the appointed time, you will be greeted by staff who will ask you for your coats and wraps, remind you to silence or leave your mobile phones and other devices, and direct you to a holding room or reception area where you will have a chance to mix and mingle with others who are waiting to be presented to the host and special guests. The reception area may be the room for the cocktail party, which leaves you free to meet and greet others. (For more information, see the section **Mixing and Mingling** in **Chapter 5. Cocktail Party Manners** and the section **Meeting and Greeting** in **Chapter 6. Manners in Business Settings**.)

At some point, you will be invited to join the receiving line. At the beginning of the receiving line, you may be asked to state your name and title or hand in your business card or the card that was sent with the invitation so that your name will be properly given to the first person on the receiving line. In other situations, you will be expected to introduce yourself to the first person and to each person in the line. Take the hand of each person in the receiving line and shake it clearly and firmly—without being forceful—and engage in very brief small talk, saying, "Thank you for the invitation" (where appropriate) or, "It is a pleasure to be here this evening." Keep in mind there are other people waiting behind you to join the receiving line. If you know the people on the line personally, you will know what to say that is appropriate and relevant to the situation.

At some very formal dinners, there may not be a receiving line if the host prefers to mix and mingle with guests and talk to them in a less formal style. If that is the case, be prepared for the host to join your conversation, shake your hand, say something personally to you, or otherwise engage with you. Being prepared for this situation by keeping a cocktail in your left hand and your right hand free will facilitate the situation. Consider also what you might want to say to your host so that he appreciates your presence. If you do not get a chance to meet the host, do not worry. Some hosts will circulate during the dinner to make sure that they meet and greet everyone. Others do not have a chance to meet everyone, especially if the crowd is large and there is little space to circulate.

Look for the tray of drinks passed at formal parties

Once you have been presented to the host—and the special guests, if any—you will normally be offered a drink and the opportunity to circulate among the other guests during the cocktail part of the meal. If the formal event is large, you will be in an ample room with plenty of staff circulating with hors d'oeuvres and trays of prepared drinks. You can also ask for a drink you want, and the staff will bring it to you or point you toward the bar. Remember to avoid eating any messy foods and take napkins when offered. You should also eat your hors d'oeuvres immediately so that you can dispose of any items you don't want to hold. That way, you keep your right hand free for shaking hands and trading business cards. (For more information about how to participate in cocktail parties, see **Chapter 5. Cocktail Party Manners**.)

At some point in the evening, you will be invited into the dining room and provided with seating instructions unless you learned them by picking up a card indicating your table number. When you get to your table, arrange the seating with your dining partners, unless place cards indicate where you should sit. If the very formal dinner is small—less than twenty-four people—you may be seated at one long table and your place indicated with a handwritten place card. Do not change the seating. At small tables—depending on the size and diameter—you'll have a chance to chat with the people to your left, right, and across the table. If you can easily hear your dinner companions across the table, you should feel free to talk with them, but if you must strain to hear, limit yourself to chatting with the people to your left or to your right. At one large table (typically relatively wide), you will be expected to chat only with your neighbor to the left or the right, but not across from you.

Look for your place cards to determine where you should sit

When you sit down, you will find a place card and a place plate, also called a charger, which is used to display elegant china too valuable and too large to be used for eating. These chargers are typically removed before the first course, but they make a beautiful setting and show the dining table to good advantage when guests arrive in the dining room. The presence of place plates also indicates to guests that professional staff will be serving dinner, since staff members will remove the chargers before the meal.

Being Served in Very Formal Settings

In very formal dinners, as at many white tablecloth restaurants, you will be expected to participate in each course when presented, whether by serving yourself from platters presented on your left side (butler service), being served by staff from platters on your left (Russian service), or being presented with plated dishes (American style), normally served from the left. Staff members who serve you butler style will give you the appropriate serving utensils, if necessary. In Russian service, the staff member will serve you from a platter or serving dish by holding the platter in his left hand and serving you with his right hand. This way, the wait staff can give you what you want after you indicate which food item(s) you want and how many while also ensuring there is plenty of food for everyone. During the meal, your plates will be removed from the right side, the opposite of the serving side. Your water glass and the appropriate wine glass will be filled with the appropriate wine or beverage for the next course, normally before the food is served. In these very formal occasions, you are expected to ignore—and not comment on—the service, since formal service is designed to be unobtrusive. You should, instead, focus on the conversation at the table. If asked about your food choices or beverage choices, then it is appropriate to respond—in a friendly manner—to the staff member.

In addition, flatware will be presented as needed just before the next course is served. In fact, even in very formal settings, it is unusual to have more than three forks, three spoons, and two knives at each place setting. If there is a need for more, then the flatware is brought to the table on a platter or salver and then placed in front of you on either the left—if a fork—or the right—if a knife or spoon. When the presentation is being made, do not help the staff member. The individual is trained to do it correctly, and your inter-ference only makes the process more difficult. Just before the flatware is being presented (placed in front of you at the correct location), the unused flatware from the previous course will be removed.

While the simple use of forks, knives, and spoons is probably clear, there are lots of other utensils that may be new to you. The first rule of behavior when confronting unu-sual flatware or utensils of any kind is not to draw attention to the situation. The second is to observe your host to see what it might be used for and how it should be used. Watching and waiting can save you from some embarrassing situations, such as eating salad with the fish fork and fish knife or thinking that the fingerbowl is a soup bowl. Some of the unusual utensils you might encounter include:

- **Butter pick:** fork-like utensil for removing the butter (whether in rolls or butter pats) from a butter dish
- **Cocktail fork** (also called a seafood fork): a small narrow fork with short tines used to separate seafood from snail, scallop, mussel, or clam shells
- **Demitasse spoon:** a very small spoon used with small coffee cups to blend the sugar or milk or cream with the coffee
- **Fish fork:** a fork with a wider left tine to separate the flesh of the fish from the bones
- **Fish knife:** a knife with a wide blade and a niche in the side that is used to sepa-rate the fish bones from the flesh

- **Grapefruit spoon:** a thin spoon with a pointed tip, and sometimes a serrated side, to eat citrus fruits segmented and served in the original grapefruit or orange skin
- **Ice cream fork:** a fork that looks like a spoon with short tines and a wide bowl to carry ice cream to the mouth
- **Ice cream spoon:** a spoon with a very wide and shallow bowl used for ice cream and other frozen desserts
- **Iced tea spoon:** a long-handled spoon used to stir iced tea so that the lemon or sugar get well mixed
- **Lobster fork:** a narrow, single or two-tined fork used to remove meat from the shell of a lobster
- **Nutcracker:** a two-sided instrument with hinge used to crack open nuts such as almonds, walnuts, pecans, and hazelnuts
- **Nut pick:** a thin, toothpick-like instrument used to remove nut meats from the shells
- **Olive fork:** a long-handled and long-tined fork used to move olives from a dish to your plate so that they can be picked up by a regular fork and eaten
- **Olive picker:** a multiple-tined tong-like instrument used to remove olives from a jar or deep bowl without having to use your hands
- **Oyster fork:** a small wide-tined fork used for eating oysters
- **Pickle fork:** a small fork with long tines used to remove pickles from a central pickle dish and place them on your plate
- **Strawberry fork:** a fork with three long tines made to spear or pierce a fresh strawberry and hold it while dipping it in sugar, sauce, or cream before putting on the plate to eat with a different fork
- **Salt spoon:** a very small spoon used to take salt from saltcellars (small containers of salt used instead of saltshakers) and sprinkle it on the food
- **Sugar tongs:** a pair of tongs used to remove sugar cubes from a bowl to your coffee or tea

Because the flatware will be presented for each course, you will not have any extra forks, knives, and spoons. In that case, you will know what to use. Act as if you have seen the flatware before and know what to do with it; then, watch other guests closely so that you can see what they do. If what they do makes sense, follow their example. If not, watch your host closely. He will show the correct procedure. In most cases, unusual flatware is simply a different size or shape from what you are used to using. The oyster and lobster forks are smaller than dinner forks and have a different shape and arrangement of the tines, but you use them in similar ways. Eating an oyster from the shell with a large dinner fork would be awkward and sloppy; there is a reason for the oyster fork.

Guests at very formal dinner parties are provided with a range of courses, each served separately and designed to balance the menu and complement the previous and following courses. A formal dinner will include at least seven courses—each accompanied by appropriate wines—which normally include the following:

- Appetizer
- Soup
- Fish
- Intermezzo or other palate cleanser
- Main course with vegetables and other accompaniments
- Cold dish or salad
- Dessert

Depending on the tastes of the host, traditions of an establishment, or other aspects of the formal dinner, the courses may vary. Sometimes, the salad is served as an appetizer and a cheese course is served instead of the cold dish or salad course. At other times, the fish course is eliminated in favor of adding a cheese course.

As the number of courses increases, the size of the portions decreases so that guests can enjoy each course without becoming too full. Consider the following options when deciding which courses to keep or eliminate:

- Appetizer course
- Soup course
- Fish course
- Intermezzo course
- Main course
- Salad course
- Cheese course
- Dessert course
- Savory course

The intermezzo is a course served between two other courses—typically between the fish course and the entrée, or main course—in order to clear the palate and prepare you for the flavors of the main dish. Sometimes, however, an intermezzo is served between the main course and the dessert course. If the salad is served at this time, it serves the same function. A cheese course can be added as well. In the United States, the cheese course tends to be served after the meal or as an alternate dessert; in France, it is often served before the dessert. Restaurants in the United States who follow the French model serve the salad after the main course; however, many United States restaurants offer a salad as an alternative appetizer or as a course that follows the appetizer courses and precedes the main course. It keeps diners busy while the kitchen prepares the main courses.

Five-course formal dinners include either an appetizer or soup course and eliminate the fish course. A typical five-course formal meal consists of the following:

- Appetizer or soup
- Intermezzo or other palate cleanser
- Main course with vegetables and other accompaniments
- Salad
- Dessert

For each of these courses, separate pieces of flatware will be placed on the table before the course is served, or in some cases—such as the first course—placed on the table before you arrive.

Use your finger bowl to clean your fingers between courses at very formal dinners

Very formal dinner parties may require use of a finger bowl. Staff will present it between courses if the courses involved the use of fingers or if the food has been awkward to eat. Typically served slightly warm, the water often contains a lemon or lime, and the finger bowl holding the water is placed on a plate, accompanied by a clean napkin. Using the finger bowl involves dipping the fingers into the bowl to cleanse them and then drying your fingers delicately with the clean napkin, which gets placed back on the table beside the plate holding the finger bowls. After you use the finger bowl, the professional staff will remove the bowl, plate, and napkin. A finger bowl may also be used at the end of a meal to allow guests to refresh their fingers.

At the conclusion of the meal, the host will invite the group to move to another room for a performance or other entertainment. That cue is your invitation to leave the table, whether you have finished or not, and move to the other room, thanking your dinner companions for a lovely discussion as you walk.

If you must leave at this point, take a moment to thank your host if you can. This conversation may not be possible because the host may be escorting the guest(s) of honor to the other room or may be are otherwise detained. You may also have trouble thanking your hosts at a large very formal event because they may disappear before the evening is over or the crowds may make saying good night very awkward. Therefore, the handwritten personal note becomes even more important as a way to show your appreciation. Complete and mail a handwritten note, on high-quality card stock, within a day or two of the event. (For more information about thank you notes, see the sections **Thank You, Thank You Notes,** and **Thank You Presents** in **Chapter 2. Conduct Becoming a Guest.**) If you're traveling or otherwise unable to write and mail it promptly, still send it, even if it is late.

CHAPTER 9

Enjoying Yourself

—◁∞∞▷—

"But that's the whole aim of civilization: to make everything a source of enjoyment."
—Leo Tolstoy, *Anna Karenina*

Table manners are a matter of comfort and graciousness, so learning and using them can help you enjoy a wide range of situations. Knowing basic good behavior beyond table manners will help you to enjoy an event with others and help others enjoy the event as well. These guidelines will help you take even more pleasure in special occasions with new acquaintances, colleagues, and friends.

Monitoring Voice Tone and Volume

Part of enjoying yourself at a dinner party is speaking in a respectful manner that encourages conversation, which means modulating your voice. Whether you are in a nice restaurant or a private home, you need to pay attention to your tone of voice, volume, and pace of speaking.

Tone of voice can make a big difference in a conversation. A strident, condescending, or critical tone can put people off and inhibit their ability to hear what you are saying. Therefore, consider how you make your points during conversation. Making statements in a firm and friendly manner contributes to the discussion and enhances the evening. As long as your tone indicates that you respect the other guests and their opinions, even forceful debates can be wonderful evening conversation. Making bold pronouncements without listening to others makes people uncomfortable and detracts from the quality and ease of the discussion. Criticizing ideas viciously, berating individuals, and speaking in a condescending manner can turn a potentially great evening sour.

The second aspect to consider is the volume of your voice. Pay attention to your voice and think about whether it is too soft or too loud; then you can change the volume to fit the room and the needs of your fellow diners. If a fellow guest is speaking too quietly or too loudly, feel free to ask her in a respectful and friendly manner to change her voice volume. This request can be a gift to her and everyone at the dinner party.

Adjust your voice volume if background noise in the room where you are dining requires it, but don't hesitate to ask your host or the restaurant to turn the music down. Alternatively, you can ask to be moved to a quieter table at a restaurant. At a dinner party, suggest that you move to a different chair. There is nothing more frustrating than not being able to hear the conversation because of too much background noise, and any host would be glad to make changes so that each guest can be part of the conversation.

Your pace of speaking can also affect your fellow diners' ability to listen and understand what you are saying. Talking too fast—especially if you have an accent—can prevent clear communication, and talking too slowly can bore people and cause their minds to wander. Pay attention to how quickly you speak, and adjust your style if you think you should. If someone else at the table speaks too fast or too slow, ask them nicely to alter the pace of their talking.

Using Language with Care

Because eating a meal with other people is, by definition, a social experience, you should be careful about the language you use and its potential impact on your dinner companions. Using people's actual names and pronouncing them correctly is the first principle of good language use. Because there is nothing sweeter than the sound of your name pronounced carefully and positively, remember to use other people's names correctly. You will set a good tone and help everyone at the table remember their fellow diners' names.

The second principle is to avoid using profane language or other words that do not belong in dining situations. Say what you want at home or in private situations, but monitor your language in restaurants or at dinner parties in someone's home. After all, you don't want to lose a chance to make new friends, to be considered for a job opportunity or a possible promotion, or to expand your range of acquaintances because you cannot control your language.

A third aspect of language use involves sensitivity to others. Cultural expectations about language have changed a lot in the last ten years; many words and labels that used to be common are no longer acceptable or appropriate for polite company. They often carry pejorative connotations that may or may not be intended. Words that discriminate against groups of people—whether ethnic, religious, racial, or sexual—and jokes that make others cringe in embarrassment are not acceptable. Learn to avoid them.

Dressing to Enjoy Yourself

Deciding what to wear to various events can be an opportunity and a challenge. When in doubt, ask the host about the dress code if you are going to a private dinner party. If you are planning to go to a restaurant, call and ask what to wear. While most restaurants are moving toward informal dress codes, many quality restaurants encourage "smart casual," and some white tablecloth restaurants encourage or require jacket and tie (and equivalent for women). Others require collar shirts (and the equivalent for women) to discourage t-shirts. Investigate the dress code so you don't stick out or feel uncomfortable at your event. You don't want to be overdressed or underdressed.

Dress to feel pleased with your outfit

Dress in a manner that reflects well on you. Often that means dressing up a bit more than you normally do. Remember that your appearance reflects both positively and negatively on you, depending on what you are wearing. As Kate Spade has advised, "Showing an appreciation for time and place are reflected first in your appearance; it's often what leaves a lasting impression, as well. Personal grooming and style are your calling card wherever you go." People will often remember what you wear and how you look, so dress to make a positive impression.

Choose clothes that make you feel good about yourself. After all, you are attending a private dinner party or going out to a restaurant to enjoy yourself. Even if you're attending a business-related event, wearing clothes that make you feel good improves your ability to be sociable.

Wear something that complements the evening, makes you look particularly smart, and enables you to feel pleased with what you are wearing. This advice means men should not wear hats—especially not baseball caps—in restaurants or at dinner parties, and women should not wear revealing outfits or loads of jewelry that make other people feel uncomfortable. Dining together is about respecting and enjoying the people around you, not ruining their evening with inappropriate clothing and accessories.

Managing Personal Space

Recognizing your need for personal space and showing consideration for the personal space of others will also make your dinner party run more smoothly.

Personal space refers to the distance between yourself and someone else, and it is a mark of respect for the other person to recognize what space he wants or needs. Some people are comfortable being very close to another person and are happy touching or hugging, while others demand some room between them and another person. Try to determine how much personal space others need. Remember to distinguish the differences in personal space between you and your family and you and your colleagues.

Determining the amount of space another person needs is very simple. If you feel tension or awkwardness with someone, simply ask him what space separation makes him comfortable, and most people will tell you. Or watch what happens when you inadvertently move into this person's space. If you infringe on his space and cause him to shrink from further conversation, some of the social pleasure of the occasion evaporates.

Those who have eaten in crowded urban restaurants know the challenges of maintaining privacy and respecting personal space when sitting very close to other people at a nearby table. In fact, urban dwellers are very good at preserving their space in such difficult surroundings. Those attending restaurants in more rural or suburban areas—or attending fancy, elegant restaurants—expect more space between their table and others.

Treating Restaurants with Respect

Part of enjoying yourself at a restaurant involves treating the staff members with respect. Unfortunately, some diners feel that because they are paying for dinner, they can treat the staff any way they like, and they are often callous, condescending, and critical. Ironically, wait staff are trained to provide attentive service and consider what guests would like. Having good manners means treating the person waiting on you with respect and even admiration for the many tasks necessary to make your meal a pleasurable, error-free event.

The first place to show respect is in making, changing, and cancelling restaurant reservations. When making reservations—in person, by telephone, or through an online reservation service—provide all the details necessary for the event and confirm them twice to avoid any possible errors. If you need to change, postpone, or cancel your reservation, communicate with the restaurant as soon as possible so that it can make appropriate adjustments. Making reservations at several restaurants for the same night is a common but offensive activity because it prevents the restaurant from booking all possible tables. Making several reservations and cancelling all but one at the last minute is also rude and inconsiderate. Not cancelling the other restaurants is even more egregious.

A second way to show your good manners is to show up on time for your reservation. Restaurant staff members have held a table for you, and if they are doing many turns—seating different parties throughout the evening—they may need that table at another time. With some exceptions, that table is not yours for the evening. The normal length of time for a decent restaurant meal is approximately two hours, thereby enabling a restaurant to seat another party either before or after your reservation.

A third aspect of treating staff members with courtesy is to avoid making a scene for any reason, whether the party has been drinking too much, enjoying the drama of the evening, or acting loudly and haughtily. There is no call for this behavior; it simply reflects badly on everyone in the party, regardless of who exhibits such atrocious behavior.

Wait staff is trained to serve on your left side and clear on your right side (Lower Left and Raise Right), so remember to move out of the way when food is being brought to the table or being cleared. Your awareness can help the wait staff do their job properly.

The most important part of good manners in restaurant settings, however, is the way in which you treat the staff members who serve you food and beverages and cater to your desires. Treating them like human beings will go a long way to providing you with a great evening. As Colleen Rush, author of *The Mere Mortal's Guide to Fine Dining*, has written: "Show your genuine appreciation and interest, or even cluelessness—by asking questions, encouraging suggestions, and complimenting the staff's efforts—and you will have an extraordinary experience. Restaurant staff love to strut their stuff, and they will go out of their way to dazzle inquisitive and polite diners." The evening will be more pleasant and the service will be smoother and more attentive, regardless of the level of the restaurant, if you speak to the wait staff with respect. Calling them "Honey," "Darling," "Hey," or "Sweetie" does not endear you to them nor does it establish a respectful relationship. Clapping or whistling for service is no better. Treating them like people working hard to make your meal special will make a positive difference in the evening and in your enjoyment.

Calling wait staff by name (which you may know, since many servers introduce themselves by name) or waving delicately and politely to summon them (rather than clapping or whistling) is an effective way to obtain their attention and ask for the service or items you want. Knowing their names also helps you get their attention if you have a problem with food or service.

If you have a problem with the service or the food, mention it to your server so that it can be remedied. You have a right to expect good service appropriate to the restaurant you are frequenting. If you have guests at your table and wish to protect them from an awkward conversation, excuse yourself and talk to the server—or the manager—in a quiet corner. After all, the restaurant wants you to have a good experience so you'll return and recommend it to others. Holding back on your criticism in order to dump it in an online review is unhelpful, insensitive, and poor manners on your part. If you had a wonderful evening, praising the restaurant online (whether in a review on Yelp or Urbanspoon or on the restaurant's Facebook page) is a wonderful way to show your appreciation. It can also make a real difference to the success of the restaurant, since social media is increasingly driving traffic to restaurants.

Tipping

Tipping is a common practice in United States restaurants for many reasons. Most servers in all but the finest restaurants are paid an hourly wage that is below the normal minimum wage. Tips are part of their income. Tips also acknowledge the quality of their service. While the range for ordinary decent service is 15 to 20 percent—with 15 percent indicating good service and 20 percent indicating excellent service—customers at a fine dining restaurant or those who have received excellent service leave even more. Many restaurant bills now come with tip calculations of 15, 18, and 20 percent, which help you with the calculations. Remember also that the 15 to 20 percent should be based on what the meal costs (adding back in the value of any coupons or other discount procedures).

Otherwise, the tip you leave is considerably less than the normal 15 to 20 percent of the total bill.

Even if you're not satisfied with your service, you should still leave a tip for the server because it a significant part of her income. When the service is poor, most people leave 10 to 15 percent and sometimes less, thereby indicating that the service was substandard but appreciating that the person needs an income. However, you should explain the problems with service, sharing your perceptions in a friendly tone with the server and, if the server will not listen or does not care, with the manager and offering your feedback as a way to help your waiter improve the service in the future. Because you went to the restaurant to enjoy yourself, finding ways to help the restaurant change will ensure that you will enjoy it more in the future.

When you go to a restaurant with friends, you will probably split the bill with each person—or couple—sharing the bill equally. However, sometimes individuals—or couples—want to divide the bill according to what each person ordered and drank. While this division may be more realistic and accurate, often it destroys the tenor of the evening and creates difficulties among the people at the table. Since paying for the bill comes at the end of the evening—when some guests are tired and some may have had several drinks—it can be a time fraught with difficulty. One way to avoid this awkward situation is to clarify what the practice will be ahead of time. Then it is easier to ask for separate bills—something most restaurant staff members are happy to provide.

Pleasures of the Table and the Evening

The purpose of dining with friends, family, or colleagues is the enjoyment of the event, so it is important to understand what is involved in creating an experience of pleasure. When you invite people to dinner, you do so to provide them with a happy experience. When someone thanks you for the evening, they often say how much they enjoyed themselves.

According to Lionel Tiger, author of *The Pursuit of Pleasure*, there are four aspects of a good meal with good company—physiological, social, psychological, and aesthetic. Physiological pleasure comes from sensory delight—the texture of the table linens, the quality of the paper used in the menu, the flavors of the food, and the taste of the beverages. Savoring the food and wine increases this aspect of pleasure and contributes joy to the evening. Just think about how dinner guests discuss the food, its ingredients, and the way it was prepared.

You can enhance the physiological pleasure of good food by practicing the full process of tasting. Although most people don't realize it, human beings taste their food first with their eyes. Therefore, when presented with food on a plate, look at it carefully. Note how it is presented and ask yourself what you might have done differently. Examining it carefully first—although not to the extent of making yourself or your companions at dinner uncomfortable—tends to increase your interest in what it will smell and taste like, all aspects of increasing the pleasure of the meal.

The second step is to smell the food. What is the dominant aroma? Does it have no aroma? What did you think it would smell like? What contributes to the aroma? What are the ingredients that produce this delicious combination of aromas? This process of thinking about the dish will help you determine its dominant ingredients just from its aroma. Then actually taste the food, thinking about what you are eating. What does it taste like in the front of the mouth? Does it change its flavor as you chew it? How does it taste as you swallow it? What is the texture like? How is the texture different from what you expected? Paying close attention to taste enhances the pleasure of the meal and the physiological rewards that come with fine dining. This three-step process—look, smell, taste—can be used with any meal at a dinner party or in any restaurant.

Social pleasure involves the delight of being with friends, family, and colleagues during an evening. It is the enjoyment of other people. Spending time when you can focus attention on them and really listen, enjoying their company without having to do anything else, adds a special dimension of joy to the evening. Being in a comfortable setting also produces social pleasure.

Psychological pleasure comes from accomplishing a task or fulfilling a goal. With a dinner party, just being invited can bring a sense of happiness. Thinking about a future party can make someone feel good. And the host will feel good planning, organizing, and making the evening a success. In the same way, discovering a new restaurant, preparing a new dish, presenting food in a new way, or finding a great food and wine pairing all contribute to the pleasures associated with an event. Even finding the right host or hostess present (See **Chapter 3. Conduct Becoming a Guest**)—and one that just seems to be the perfect gift for the occasion—can create a good feeling. In a restaurant, trying a new food item—or ordering something you don't fully understand—and finding that you like it can also bring delight. Even practicing good manners throughout a difficult evening can bring a sense of accomplishment and psychological pleasure.

Enjoy the beauty of champagne

The aesthetic observation of a beautiful table setting, presentation of food on the plate, and menu design can trigger pleasure, as can an interesting and lively conversation. Very similar to the pleasure derived from noticing a work of art, a beautiful landscape, or a scene from nature, this form of pleasure brings joy to many people. Being part of an event that makes you notice and appreciate the creative elements of the evening contributes to this form of pleasure. Your internal awareness of how beautiful things are—how you have relished the conversation, the visual aspects of the event, and the ideas—are all aspects of this form of pleasure.

Thank you for reading this book. We hope that you will refer to it often; discuss it with colleagues, family, and friends; and continue to observe and practice good manners. As Nicholas Clayton, a professional butler, has written, "Eating should be fun and not a time for worrying about which knife and fork to use, and the easiest way to allay those fears is to learn how to eat with style and perfect etiquette." Now that you know what good manners are, you can make your life easier and increase your enjoyment of a wide range of social situations, the most delightful of which are an evening of good food, good beverages, and intriguing conversation with good people.

Enjoy the pleasures of the evening

Works Cited

Baldridge, Letitia. *Letitia Baldridge's New Complete Guide to Executive Manners*. New York: Rawson Associates/Macmillan, 1993.

Claiborne, Craig. *Elements of Etiquette: A Guide to Table Manners in an Imperfect World*. New York: Morrow, 1992.

Clayton, Nicholas. *A Butler's Guide to Table Manners*. London: National Trust Press, 2007.

Culinary Institute of America. *Remarkable Service: A Guide to Winning and Keeping Customers for Servers, Managers, and Restaurant Owners*. New York: Wiley, 2001.

Dahmer, Sondra J., and Kurth W. Kahl. *Restaurant Service Basics*. New York: Wiley, 2002.

Franco, Angela Marie. *The Table Manners Coach: A Lifestyle Perspective for Comfort and Poise in Any Dining Situation*. New York: AMF Direct, 2012.

Garner, Curtrise. *The New Rules of Etiquette: A Young Woman's Guide to Style and Poise at Work, at Home, and On the Town*. Avon, Mass.: Adams Media, 2009.

Inch, Arthur, and Arlene Hirst. *Dinner Is Served: An English Butler's Guide to the Art of the Table*. New York: MJF Books (Fine Communication), 2003.

Kirkham, Mike, Peggy Weiss, and Bill Crawford. *The Waiting Game: The Essential Guide for Wait Staff*. Berkeley: Ten Speed Press, 2002.

KRC Research. *Civility in America 2013*. www.webershandwick.com or www.pwelltate.com accessed April 2014.

Kryston, Jill Evans. "Vignettes on Etiquette: Important Information You Should Know about Manners," www.definingmanners.comhttp://www.definingmanners.com/

Lininger, Mike, ed., "Placing Glassware," *Etiquette Scholar* www.etiquettescholar.com/dining_etiquette/table_setting/place_setting/glassware_and_stemware/place_stemware.htmlhttp://www.etiquettescholar.com/dining_etiquette/table_setting/place_setting/glassware_and_stemware/place_stemware.html

Long, Sheila M. *The Little Book of Etiquette*. New York: Barnes and Noble, 2000.

Mackay, Ian. *Food for Thought: Being a Compendium of Culinary Quips, Quotes, Anecdotes, Facts and Recipes by the Great and Not-So-Great*. Freedom, Calif.: The Crossing Press, 1995.

Manners, Judith. *Miss Manners' Guide to Excruciatingly Correct Behavior*. New York: Warner Books, 1982.

Mintz, Corey. *How to Host a Dinner Party*. Toronto: House of Anansi, 2013.

Post, Peggy, Anna Post, Lizzie Post, and Daniel Post Senning. *Emily Post's Etiquette*. 18th edition. New York: Morrow, 2011.

Post, Peter. *Emily Post's Essential Manners for Men: What to Do, When to Do It, and Why.* New York: Morrow, 2012.

Rosen, Lynn. *Elements of the Table: A Simple Guide for Hosts and Guests.* New York: Clarkson Potter, 2007.

Rossi, Patricia. *Everyday Etiquette: How to Navigate 101 Common and Uncommon Social Situations.* New York: St. Martin's Griffin, 2011.

Rush, Colleen. *The Mere Mortal's Guide to Fine Dining: From Salad Forks to Sommeliers, How to Eat and Drink in Style without Fear of Faux Pas.* New York: Broadway, 2006.

Spade, Kate. *Manners: Always Gracious, Sometimes Irreverent.* New York: Simon and Schuster, 2004.

Tiger, Lionel. *The Pursuit of Pleasure.* New Brunswick: Transaction Publishers, 2008.

Tower, Jeremiah. *Table Manners: How to Behave in the Modern World and Why Bother.* New York: Farrar, Straus and Giroux, 2016.

Vanderbilt, Amy. *Amy Vanderbilt's Etiquette: A Guide to Gracious Living by the Foremost Authority on Manners Today.* Revised edition. New York: Doubleday, 1972.

Whitmore, Jacqueline. *Business Class: Etiquette Essentials for Success at Work.* New York: St. Martin's Press, 2005.

Whitmore, Jacqueline. *How to Dine in Style: The Art of Entertaining 1920.* Oxford: Bodleian Library, 2013.

Acknowledgments

———✦———

We want to thank Linda Gold, who has generously tolerated Michael's time spent away from her while we created this book. Her positive encouragement, excellent manners, and sense of humor have been an inspiration for both of us during this project. In addition, she entertains with grace and style and always makes guests comfortable.

We also honor a number of people—Letitia Baldridge, Craig Claiborne, Nicholas Clayton, Arthur Inch, Judith Manners, Emily Post, Lynn Rosen, Kate Spade, Amy Vanderbilt, and others—who have written books about manners and etiquette. Their comments, their approaches, and their advice have assisted us in creating this book.

We were lucky that a number of colleagues and friends discussed the topic of manners with us or read various chapters, and we thank them for their advice and wise counsel. They were helpful, encouraging, and insightful. The book is better for your help. Thank you Elliott Auerbach, Kristin Backhaus, Gerald Benjamin, Sandy Christian, Terri Shand Colucci, Ted Clark, Richard Croce, Fran Divine, Gail Gallerie, Mike Hein, Patrice Huart, Angela Klopstech, Myron Koltuv, Susie Kraat, Karen Lieberman, Jodie Longto, Joie Mayo, Judy Reichler, Adele Reiter, Ann Rodman, and Susan Scherr.

Two particular people edited the entire text, and the book would not be so clear if it were not for the careful reading, comments, and advice of Dr. Karen Lieberman and James H. Ottaway, Jr. Their commitment to the book, their sensitivity to what we were trying to do, and their friendly suggestions have improved the quality of the information and the ease of reading it. We are indebted to them for their hard work and their faith in the importance of this book.

We also want to thank the many people who let us take their pictures and who made suggestions for what should be included in the book. We invited suggestions for pet peeves from our FaceBook pages, LinkedIn correspondents, and our friends and colleagues. In addition, Linda Gold, Fred Mayo, Barbara Sides, Joe Trapani, and Shara and

David Wightman lent us their china, crystal, flatware, and dining rooms for pictures. Fortessa China lent us a range of new china, flatware, and crystal. The Sides, the Wightmans, the DeRosas, the Alonsos, the Kureks, and the Randalls lent us their homes for pictures; Debra Dooley and Claire Winslow, of The Would Restaurant, let us hire their chef to prepare food and lent us their dining rooms and party pavilion to take pictures.

A number of individuals served as models; their presence, smiles, and delight in being able to show off bad manners made this whole project lots of fun for both them and us. They have also let us use their environments, equipment, and actions to show both bad and good manners. We could not have done it without all of their support. They include: Michael Aiello, Anna Alonzo, Joseph Alonzo, Ece Aytulun, Gamte Dent Arslan, Cemile Atay, Laine Barton, Irem Bayraktar, Omar Bakaner, Caner Bayraktar, Samantha Bove, Kathy Braddon, Gabrielle Brown, Dane Brown, Hugh Brown, Berk Muste Caplioglu, Olivia Casa, Randy Casarrobias, Hasan Behron Celiktas, Aimee Chen, Studio Stu Chernoff, Alp Ciryi. Samuel Davies, David DeHoff, Irena Demchenko, Anthony DiGregorio, Megan Donahue, Maurice Dorsey, Marie-Louise Enderle, Robert Enderle, Evgin Eraslaw, Selin Erkan, Erman Erturhan, Ali Eyuboglu, Yigit Eyuboglu, Ezra Favas, Armagan Fererci, Stephanie Ferndandez, Grace Gates, Rachel George, Linda Gold, Gregory Gordon, Ryan J. Graham, Cansu Gun, Penny Hays, Michael Hein, Jesse Hicks, Genieve Hudson, Mar Jahan, Kimberly Kallansrude, William Koenig, Frank Kraat, Susie Kraat, David Krikun, Virginia Leitner, Robert Leitner, Haoran Liu, Yifu Liu, Han Li, Krystal Ann Lollys, Peter M. Loughran, Cahir D. McCoole, Sandra Mary McCoole, Joan McDonald, James McDonald, Julie McDonald, Aditya Malladi, Andrea Menchero, Caroline Menchero, Cesar J. Menchero, Melissa Menchero, Betul Mentese, Lisa Metz, Howard Mont, Betsy Lichtshein Mont, Marie Nehme, Sally A. Nicholas, Stephanie Nunez, Robert Osgood, Monte Parker, Joseph Pawelczak, Darley Randall, Pinny Randall, Judith Reichler, John Rice, Sal Rossano, Claude Sampton, Irem Sayden, Jon Scoria, Mehmet Burok Sezer, Barbara Sides, David Sides, Marty Singleton, Ryan Sutherland, Elizabeth Sydney, Claudia Toffel, Elaine Walker, Martin Walker, Sofia Wang, Asher Weinman, Samuel Weinman, John R. Weisgerber, Alex Wheeler, David Wightman, Shara Wightman, Evan J. Wolff, Orhan Yesilyurt, Tanur lara Yilmat, Jiayu Zhang, and Kevin Zraly.

Albert LaFarge of the LaFarge Agency, our enthusiastic agent, kept convincing publishers that it should happen. Susan Randol of Skyhorse Publishing was a supportive, engaging, and smart editor who believed in the book and made it happen.